by Mike White

Published in the USA by:
BearManor Media
P O Box 71426
Albany, Georgia 31708
www.bearmanormedia.com

ISBN: 978-1-59393-777-5
Printed in the United States of America
Cover design by Mike White
Book design by Robbie Adkins, www.adkinsconsult.com

Table of Contents

To Skizz
Thanks for sharing the same warped sense of humor.

Acknowledgements

Thank you to all of the people who took time to help me with this project: Andrea White, Kate Hennessey, Joe Tropea, Robert St. Mary, Barbara Goodson, April Winchell, Terry Thoren, Randy Ridges, Craig Mitchell, Randy Nogg, Jim Riffel, Josh Hadley, Straw Weisman, Robert Harmon, Lloyd Kaufman, Charles Kaufman, Skizz Cyzyk, Kurt Gardner, Matthew Manjourides, Steve Pinto, Bob Buchholz, Connie Sue Cook, Andrew Leavold and Kent Skov.

The Mad Movies with the L.A. Connection cast: Steve Pinto, Stephen Rollman, Connie Sue Cook (back row), Bob Buchholz, and Kent Skov (front row).

Author's Note

Mad Movies with the L.A. Connection premiered on WDIV, Detroit's NBC affiliate, on September 13, 1985 at 7:30 p.m. Cable television had begun to make inroads into more American homes, though the industry was still in relative infancy. I was a young pup myself; only thirteen years old but already a connoisseur of comedy. *Mad Movies with the L.A. Connection* tickled my funny bone and I became slightly obsessed with the show.

After the premiere of *Mad Movies with the L.A. Connection,* the show moved to its semi-regular spot of 1 a.m. on Saturday nights (in Detroit, at least). Not wanting to miss an episode, I stayed up well past my bedtime and tuned in my thirteen-inch black and white set to the show, turning down the volume to barely audible levels so as to not wake my parents. There, in the late night glow of the cathode rays, I experienced my first foray into the world of "mock dub," a subgenre of comedy that I grew to appreciate more as the years progressed.

When Ben Ohmart of BearManor Media asked if I would be interested in writing a history of *Mad Movies with the L.A. Connection*, I jumped at the chance, recalling those viewings in the wee hours. I had been hoping to write about the show and talk to its creator, Kent Skov, and I finally got my chance to learn how everything came together and what Skov and the rest of the L.A. Connection have been up to in the intervening years.

Kent Skov

You can't explain *Mad Movies with the L.A. Connection* without discussing Kent Skov.

Skov grew up in Kentfield, California in Marin County. This area north of San Francisco produced several notable people including Robin Williams and Pete Carroll.

"I had a tape recorder that I got for Christmas as a kid," says Skov. "I would do all sorts of voices and take-offs on TV shows like *Let's Make a Deal.* I wasn't even ten years old. I didn't really get into acting until I was seventeen and had my first theater class. I got an award in class for Distinction in Drama and thought, *Boy, I didn't have to do hardly anything to get this.* My teacher told me he thought I had the ability to go on and make a living in the business, and that really gave me the confidence to do so."

After graduation, Skov attended San Francisco State College, where he joined The Committee, an offshoot of The Second City improvisational comedy troupe. Howard Hesseman (*WKRP in Cincinnati*) and David Ogden Stiers (*M*A*S*H*) had founded The Committee in 1963. "They basically had three companies. To get into one of them you had to come in on Saturday afternoon to an open workshop where there'd be anywhere from forty to sixty people. If you came to that afternoon workshop enough, and if they liked you, you'd get invited to join the group. Then, you had to get there at nine in the morning on Saturday and Sunday. As a college student, that was not a lot of fun. Plus, I had to commute from Marin over to San Francisco. Nevertheless, I loved improve, so I kept at it. When I got into one of the companies, the Committee Players, we would perform in Berkeley once a week. In about nine months, I did my first show with them, working my way through the ranks for almost two years until The Committee closed in 1972.

"I started my own improv group when I was in college and got a VJ job when I was in my senior year. *Video Radio,* a public access show, went to the 10,000 local households that had cable. It was pre-MTV, and people could see us talking and spinning records – back in those days we had records – and some reel-to-reel tapes."

Skov worked on *Video Radio* with legendary DJ Norman Davis. "I went on his show and did pantomime and comedy routines," says Skov. "He said to me, 'Look, I can't do this anymore.' He was coming right from work doing 2 p.m. to 6 p.m. and would come in to do the show at 1 a.m. and he was just exhausted. He wasn't going home in between because this was in San Francisco and he lived in Mill Valley. He offered me his spot on *Video Radio*. I had enough music for about two shows.

"I played my music during the first show and I did poetry and it was all artsy and stuff. All these people just loved it because I was playing classic Neil Young. I did that for a couple weeks and was starting to get a nice following; I mean, it was only in 10,000 houses, so how much of a following can you get? We were on MetroMedia television, which was kind of like Comcast cable was in 2014.

"Eventually, Norman told me that he'd have his daughter, Susie, get music for me, different and eclectic stuff because Norman would get all this free music sent to him because people would want to get it played. It was like delivering drugs. I'd go to his house, 'Here's your music.' One time, The Tubes—Fee Waybill—he brought a cassette and asked me to play it. I think I may have been one of the premiere guys who introduced 'White Punks on Dope.' And, a couple years later, we'd run into The Tubes again." The people who liked me for the first couple weeks were like, 'What happened to that guy?'

In addition to *Video Radio*, Skov also worked with Norman Davis at KSAN radio doing voices and impressions. "Nixon was being impeached at the time, so I started doing Nixon for him and eventually went on to do all the presidents, mainly Ronald Reagan."

Skov moved to Los Angeles in 1975, where he worked for two alumni of *The Waltons*, Ralph Waite and Will Geer. He commuted between L.A. and San Francisco, doing a two-man comedy show while continuing to work with Norman Davis. When Davis's show moved to other cities, Skov did his bits over the phone. "We have a relationship even today: he has a web series now and we still fool around doing voices."

The L.A. Connection versus the Aztec Mummy

The L.A. Connection

Before *Mad Movies and the L. A. Connection* became a television show, it played as a live event.

In 1977, Kent Skov founded the L.A. Connection comedy troupe. Skov recalls, "We grew to a pretty large repertory group pretty quickly. I started with about fifteen or sixteen people and I would take them around. We won a Whisky a Go-Go 'The Tubes' Talent Hunt' after about twenty-four hours of rehearsal with a piece called 'An Action Concerto.' It was a real physical and sound effect type piece."

The L.A. Connection was so well received that the only question many in the audience had after the troupe left the stage was how they would divide the grand prize among ten people.[1]

"Of course, I had to remind Fee Waybill that I played 'White Punks on Dope' back on *Video Radio*," says Skov. "We ended up playing with The Tubes about ten times at The Whisky A Go-Go that year. The next year, they came down to the Pantages and hired us to play with them there."

Bolstered by their victory, the L.A. Connection began performing *al fresco* in Venice Beach. They would rope off an area as a makeshift stage and busk for an average crowd of 300 people. "We had a huge homeless crowd," says Skov. "One of the homeless guys gave us a megaphone that we'd use to bark up the crowd. The crowd got so big we had to move to the center of the lawn where we were getting maybe 500 or 600 people. We added a second show and we'd get about half as many people for that one. We would have our all-stars – the top group – perform for the first show and our second tier group for the second show.

"The original core of the L.A. Connection included folks like Taylor Negron (*The Last Boy Scout*), who's still around and doing stand-up comedy, Victoria Jackson, who was on *Saturday Night Live,* and Deanna Oliver, who wrote *Casper, My Favorite Martian,* and *Animaniacs.* We had a Broadway star, Steve Tutt; he was phenomenal. One of our guys, Cork Hubbert, went on to be the elf in the UPS commercials for about two or three years. He had a pretty good series as an actor in regular sit-coms and features, too. We also had

Robin LaValley, who was on *Diff'rent Strokes* and stood in for Gary Coleman. Finally, we had Dan Weisman, who was this mogul deejay and my right-hand man and even designed our logo."

In 1978, the troupe moved indoors to open the L.A. Connection Comedy Theater at The Crossroads of the World in Hollywood, California. On May 7 of that same year, Muhammad Ali boxed a number of Hollywood stars including Richard Pryor, Marvin Gaye, Barry White, and the L.A. Connection. Later that year, they won America's Best New Comedy Group on ABC's national competition show, *America Votes on Tomorrow's Stars*, hosted by John Ritter and Joan Rivers. The following year saw the L.A. Connection perform on NBC's *Super Bowl Saturday Night* and *Make Me Laugh*, where they competed against Howie Mandel and Pat Cooper.

After a while, the troupe began to lose some of its original members. "I started having my first kind of transition in terms of the group in 1980. Most of my guys were now getting successful, going off and doing stuff. Keeping people for three years in your group was a pretty good length of time." Skov began producing *The L.A. Connection Comedy Show* for cable and opened a second theater in Sherman Oaks. "Our Saturday night show was our top improv show. We played a game on stage called Translators where I would translate someone speaking in gibberish. You teach people to translate in the intonation pattern that the person is talking as well as the emotion. You also have to hit all the pauses so that their pattern of speech matches. My background helped. As a kid I did three years of speech and phonetics. Plus, I had been doing voices and impressions."

In July 1982, Terry Thoren of the Landmark Theater chain visited the L.A. Connection and asked, "Hey, would you like to dub a movie?" Thoren ". . . approached the L.A. Connection after he saw the troupe perform a 'pre-Improvision' routine at one of its regular shows at the Sherman Oaks theater."[2]

Terry Thoren produced more than 600 episodes of animation on television. An original staff member at the Telluride Film Festival and a founder of the Denver International Film Festival, Thoren had been recruited by Landmark Theaters (America's largest art theater chain) and moved to Hollywood in 1979. Skov remembers that Thoren had heard *High Street,* a radio show in Denver, that would ask listeners

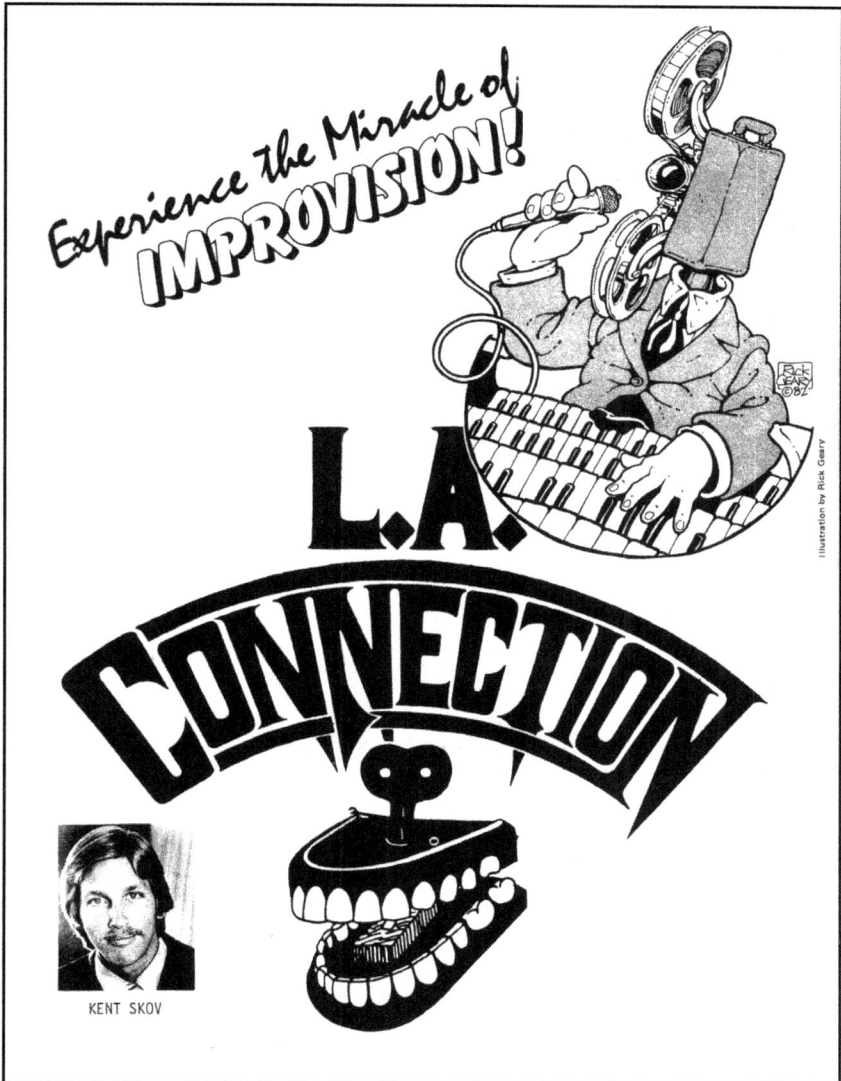

Experience the Miracle of IMPROVISION!

L.A. CONNECTION

Illustration by Rick Geary

KENT SKOV

to turn down the volume on one's TV and replace the dialogue via their broadcast.

In late August, the Fox Venice Theater hosted *The Attack of the 50 Foot Woman* with the L.A. Connection in the front row, dubbing the entire feature with their voices and reworking the campy classic into a comedy event. "We did the entire feature, which I think runs about an hour and maybe fifteen or twenty minutes. It was a big hit. Back then, we didn't have VHS, so we got a 16mm print of the film.

We could only have it about four or five days before we did the event. We put up a white sheet on the wall of my room and we ran the film repeatedly, trying to figure out what the movie was because none of us had seen it. We spent hours going over each scene, thinking about what we could say, what voices we could use, and what each scene would be about." Pressed for time, that performance proved to have more improv than any other film dub the L.A. Connection would later tackle.

Skov says, "It was a hit. KROQ radio sponsored it and they were pretty big in those days. We packed the place. The theater had about 880 seats and it sold out. We did an encore about three weeks later and sold another 600 or so tickets. We knew we had something special."

At that time, Stephen Rollman and Steve Pinto were part of the troupe. "We had April Winchell; she did both a French accent and kind of a floozy for *Attack of the 50 Foot Woman*. When we did the next movie, *Wrestling Women Versus the Aztec Mummy*, Bob Buchholz and Connie Sue Cook got involved."

"What happened was that my group was showing me through the live shows that they could write. It was training for them, too. I was the only professional writer at the time. Steve Pinto and Bob Buchholz were both from Connecticut and came out to California together. They even auditioned together. Once they started doing movies, I saw that they really could write. Bob would watch the script and make sure we didn't have any errors. He'd even check for lip synch. Connie would come up with nutty stuff that normal people don't think of and always brought a fun energy to her characters. She was probably the one who got us side-tracked. She'd go off on these stories and we'd have to bring her back. That's just part of the mind, the creative mind, that just would go and that was her strength. Steve Rollman was really good at puns and voices. He was just good at coming up with funny ideas.

"Some of them, Rollman in particular, thought they couldn't write. 'You're one of my best improvisers,' I told him. 'The difference between being an improviser and a writer is committing yourself to paper.' Once he began to realize that he could write, he became an excellent contributor. I wrote really well with all of them, but in particular, I wrote really good scripts with Bob, with Connie, and with

Attack of the 50 Foot Woman circa 1979.

Bob and Steve Rollman together. We actually wrote on another show together, and the three of us probably were, I would say, the strongest, if I had to choose the people who I worked with best. Steve Pinto had a nice sense of humor; he just didn't have my same style.

"All the while, we had to think about matching the lips. We were kind of translating our interpretation of what we thought they were saying based on the lip movement, the physical gestures, maybe the clothes they were wearing; then making them fun and utilizing them in our storytelling. Depending on the movie, we might make comments about seeing strings on spaceships like in *Plan 9 from Outer Space*. Even in some classic movies, sometimes we'd find something like they were missing a piece of their costume from one scene to another, or their hair was combed differently from one take to the next. You try to use that as a platform for your dubbing, staying within the confines of your story, as well."

When dubbing the films, the L.A. Connection would re-contextualize the on-screen action to work within the confines of a new plot. The plot might change from one screening to the next. "'We don't want to lead people on and let them think this is totally improvised,' Skov said, 'but the humor comes out of improvisation. We can take a topic in the news and use it in the plot. No two shows are the same, because five minutes into the film you know where the audience is coming from and we change the film accordingly.'"[3]

Skov recalls, "*Plan 9 from Outer Space*'s theme changed a few times. We kept it similar to the original one—you know, alien invasions, zombies, the whole kind of deal—and we just changed the dialogue a little bit and kept the story line intact. For one version, we had aliens coming down and wanting to take over an NFL franchise to dominate the sport. For one screening, I screwed up and had the same scene in the film twice. *Déjà vu!* We did the scene again and it was funnier the second time than the first because the audience was right there with us. When we did the same film the next year, I left the mistake in. It was never as funny as that first time because we all got caught off guard, too, and that's what made it funny because we were truly improvising.

"*Wrestling Women Versus the Aztec Mummy* was about setting up a big wrestling event. The guy who did it we based on Don King and called him "Joe King." Joking. He was the Asian leader of that group and then we had our guys, the promoters of this side. One year when we did it, the movie caught fire and burned. That's how old those films were: they were falling apart when we got them. For about fifteen or twenty minutes, we had to improvise in the dark, talking as the characters, until they could get the movie back up. That was pretty interesting.

"Some of the funniest moments we had were the screw-ups. On *The Hunchback of Notre Dame*, the wrong reel was taken out, so we had to improvise for twenty minutes."

"A similar predicament developed during a presentation of *Andy Warhol's Frankenstein*. 'We had planned to do the R-rated version of the movie, but the distributor sent us the X-rated version by mistake,' remembers Skov. 'Because we had screened the uncut X-rated version a couple of times prior to deciding to do the R-rated version, we were familiar with some of the additional scenes that came up. But it was a shock that we had to improvise for twenty minutes. Boy, that really threw us for a loop!'"[4]

"'We don't let the audience believe we are going in cold,' Skov said. 'We review the movie and have about four rehearsals, but when we make a mistake, that can be even more fun. Once we had a girl play both parts in *Attack of the 50 Foot Woman* of a mistress and a wife. She switched the parts by accident and the guy who played the husband said, 'You sound more and more like my wife every day.'"[5]

"In 1983, we did the international world premiere of *Cat-Women of the Moon*. KLOS Radio and *L.A. Weekly* sponsored it. We had a contest for the best cat woman outfit with a trip to Hawaii for the prize. We had a celebrity look-alike contest, as well. We had celebrities come out to judge the contest; John Helliwell of Supertramp, Catherine Bach of *Dukes of Hazzard*, Mary Woronov and Paul Bartell from *Eating Raoul* and Robert Shields from *Shields and Yarnell*. John Helliwell played with us throughout the whole event and we got a lot of coverage. That really set us up where a lot of people began to know about us. Newspapers and magazines started writing about us. Even *Entertainment Tonight* covered us. We had great audiences. We were drawing four to six hundred in lines an evening without this kind of push but that coverage really put us over the edge.

The Cat-women Contest

"This helped us to get signed with Alan Thicke to do his show, *Thicke of the Night*, in 1983. Alan Thicke had come down to one of our shows with Linda Blair. They were overdressed for our theater but we were very happy to have them and they ended up hiring us to do the 'Flicke of the Night' segment of the show.

"Connie Sue Cook and Steve Rollman wrote a lot of stuff with me for 'Flicke of the Night.' I'm not sure how much Pinto wrote on those. For voices we had Richard Belzer, Chloe Webb (who went on to play Nancy in *Sid and Nancy*), Gilbert Gottfried, Charles Fleischer (the voice of Roger Rabbit), Mike McManus, and myself.

"Before the first show went on, the head writer pulled me backstage just before we went live-to-tape. We were taping at 5:00 or 5:30 p.m., and the show aired at 11:00 or 11:30 p.m., depending on where it was syndicated. The head writer told me, 'You know, we don't think your bit is that funny so we're going to cut you back to two days a week.' Our deal was for three. I was a bit taken aback. I said, 'Oh, okay, all right. Well, I think it's pretty funny.' Now, remember, this is the head writer and a lot of the stuff the writers on that show wrote was just not very funny. Some of their sketches were funny, some weren't. Anyway, the show goes on and our bit was a huge hit.

"After the show the same writer came to me and he couldn't look me in the eye. He said, 'Fred [Silverman, the producer] and Alan really thought your bit went over well and we now want to make it five days a week.' I had gone from three in my contract down to two all the way to five before the first show even hit the air. On top of that, we got the best review in *Time* and *Newsweek*, and just about every paper raved about our segment. We had dubbed *Dr. Jekyll and Mr. Hyde* with Spencer Tracy and Ingrid Bergman. It was just unbelievable, and we had this tremendous, tremendous response."

The *Thicke of the Night* series lasted a single season. Audiences favored Johnny Carson to the mild-mannered Canadian. "*Thicke of the Night* is a muddled, repetitious, and uninteresting show whose center is inhabited by a performer of nearly stupefying dullness," wrote one reviewer.[6] "The host doesn't control the flow of the party; there's none of David Letterman's irony, Carson's crispness, Merv Griffin's precious, gossipy ardor." During this dressing down, the L.A. Connection fared well against the other show regulars. "The program's virtues include the 'Flicke of the Night' series in which Kent Skov's L.A. Connection expertly improvises comic dialogue over B-films."

According to David Hofstede's *What Were They Thinking?: The 100 Dumbest Events in Television History*, the show ". . . actually pulled a 0 share [of the ratings] in Philadelphia, which suggested the possibility that in a major metropolitan area, not one single television was tuned to the show."

On the new THICKE OF THE NIGHT show, "Flick of the Night" produced by Kent Skov, written by the L.A. Connection, gets rave reviews for premiere show!

WHAT THE CRITICS ARE SAYING ABOUT
THE L.A. CONNECTION ON THE NEW
"THICKE OF THE NIGHT" SHOW

TIME MAGAZINE/September 19

"More promising are such regular features as...
Flick of the Night, which overdubs old film
clips with irreverent irrelevancies."

BALTIMORE SUN/September 4

"The opener has a major problem with pace...But
the highpoints of this debut are really high:...
and highest of all, a hilarious re-dubbing of
several scenes from the Spencer Tracy version of
'Dr. Jekyll and Mr. Hyde'."

CINCINNATI POST/ September 5

"Perhaps the highlight of the show, the one
stunning comedy bit, is an ensemble joke about
movie soundtracks titled "Flick of the Night."

NEWSDAY/September 6

"'The Flick of the Night,' a feature in which members of the repertory company (L.A. CONNECTION)
overdub old movie footage, was the best bit of
the night...I laughed my head off at the new
script."

Critical response to Thicke of the Night

A Brief History of Mock Dubbing

To my recollection, I've never heard of that being done before where the actors would be acting one story and saying another.

It was, actually. It was done in *Gone with the Wind*. Not many people know that. Those were Japanese people, actually, and we dubbed in American voices.

— What's Up Tiger Lily?

Although many early filmmakers experimented successfully with sound, the industry's full conversion to synchronous sound trailed three decades behind the advent of motion pictures. Alfred Hitchcock's *Blackmail* (1929) begins like a typical silent film, but includes scenes of synchronous dialogue where actress Anny Ondra mouthed her lines while Joan Barry read the dialogue off screen. Even in this early "talkie," Hitchcock used sound both objectively and subjectively (the word "knife" in particular stabs at the ears of our heroine as she hears the word via an off-screen conversation).

The early days of sound were played for laughs in Stanley Donen's *Singin' in the Rain* (1952), where dialogue is slowed down, sound effects amplified, and lines meant for one actor synchronized to another. This wasn't the earliest use of sound manipulation for comic effect, but it was undoubtedly the most popular.

Ten years prior to *Singin' in the Rain*, Spaniards Antonio de Lara and Miguel Mihura took the 1936 German film *Unsterbliche Melodien* (*Immortal Melodies*) and replaced the soundtrack for comic effect. The result, *Un bigote para dos* (*A Mustache for Two*, 1940), may be one of the first feature-length films to undergo this process. Sadly, the film is believed to be lost.

The L.A. Connection's "Improvision" or "Dub-A-Vision" has roots back to early avant-garde films, as well as popular comedic entertainment, such as Jay Ward's *Fractured Flickers*, a show that shared much of its talent with *Rocky and His Friends*, including host Hans Conried and the voices of June Foray, Paul Frees, and Bill Scott.

Like *Mad Movies with the L.A. Connection*, *Fractured Flickers* was a half hour long and ran one season (1963-64). The show also featured interviews and supplied films with new, outrageous dialogue.

This same tactic was later used in Woody Allen's *What's Up, Tiger Lily?* (1966), in which two Japanese films (*International Secret Police: A Barrel of Gunpowder* and *International Secret Police: Key of Keys*) replaced their respective MacGuffins with the recipe for egg salad.

In the U.S., this practice became known as "mock dub" or "dub comedy" while the French Situationalist movement termed the same practice *détournement*. As Steve Martin said, "Those French have a different word for everything!" Practiced most notably by sinologist René Viénet, the films *Can Dialectics Break Bricks?* (1973), *The Girls of Kamare* (1974) and *Peking Duck Soup* (1977) put new, political spins on Eastern films. While railing against the unfair treatment of the proletariat by the bourgeoisie, Viénet was not above a good fart joke. Unfortunately, two other Viénet films, *L'aubergine est farcie* (*The Eggplant is Stuffed*, 1975) and *Une soutane n'a pas de braguette* (*A Cassock Has No Fly*, 1973) seem to be lost.[7]

Similar to the way Allen and Viénet used multiple sources for their work (*The Girls of Kamare*, 1974 combined *Terrifying Girls' High School: Lynch Law Classroom*, 1973 with *Female Yakuza Tale: Inquisition and Torture*, 1973), the Firesign Theater took a wide range of Republic serials, including *Adventures of Captain Marvel* (1941), *Zombies of the Stratosphere* (1952), *Undersea Kingdom* (1936), and *Captain America* (1944) for their *J-Men Forever* (1979). In addition to stitching these disparate serials together into a single narrative, new scenes of the titular J-Men were added to bridge storylines. The group would employ the same techniques in *Firesign Theater Presents 'Hot Shorts'* (1983). Around the same time as *J-Men Forever*, director Francisco Lara Polop turned *Los amantes del desierto* (*Desert Warrior*) (1957) into a comic retelling of recent events in Spain in *El asalto al castillo de la Moncloa* (1978).

The Canadian comedy show SCTV included a "mock dub" segment on their March 6, 1981, episode. "One of the most unusual *SCTV* episodes of all, featuring an actual episode of *The Cisco Kid*, season 2 episode 20, 'Sleeping Gas') with dialog written and dubbed in by Martin Short, Steve Kampmann, Peter Torokvei, and Don Dickinson. The sketch was actually a pilot for another series that

SCTV was trying to get off the ground. This entire episode was almost entirely removed from the syndicated run."[8]

Due to the popularity of the L.A. Connection's live dubbing events around California, the early 1980s included other feature-length mock dubs with *Ferocious Female Freedom Fighters* (1982) and *What's Up, Hideous Sun Demon?*[9] (1983), as well as the L.A. Connection's own *Reefer Madness II: The True Story* (1985).

Ferocious Female Freedom Fighters

Directed by Charles Kaufman, brother of Lloyd Kaufman, the co-founder of Troma Entertainment, *Ferocious Female Freedom Fighters* stemmed from Jopi Burnama's *Perempuan Bergairah* (*Passionate Woman*). Charles Kaufman and Creative Consultant Straw Weisman penned the new dialogue.

"Creative Consultant? Fuck that!" says Weisman, "I co-wrote it with Charles. We sat in his apartment over on the Upper West Side. I was a sometimes writing partner with Charles Kaufman in the mid-to late-'70s. We had written a movie called *The Outdoorsters*, which was later known as *When Nature Calls* (1985), and around that time, Lloyd made a deal with Raam Punjabi from Parkit Films and wound up with this title that we intended to do a *What's Up Tiger Lily* to. Because we were writing together, Charles asked if I wanted to do this one as well."

Charles Kaufman remembers, "When they asked me how I could make this film better, I told them that maybe they could release it without the soundtrack. If not that, then the visuals."

According to Lloyd Kaufman, "We felt it would be much better to have my brother, Charles Kaufman, who produced *Mother's Day* and *When Nature Calls*, rewrite this entirely and make it into more of a Troma movie. We changed the Rambo-type kickboxing hero into an Elvis impersonator. We changed the lady in the film, who was a serious Indonesian heroine, into a Jewish momma-type of person. We added some excellent Troma farting and other sophisticated elements."

Charles Kaufman continues, "Straw Weisman and I wrote it in about two to three weeks. It was an interesting exercise because you had to time how long the people spoke and fit your words to that."

Weisman adds, "Doing this kind of writing is harder than writing a plain old screenplay. First, you have a visual storyline and the dialogue that was already written. The story, as written, was about a female fighter, who had to fight to save her brother. It was kind of a crooked boxing movie. Our goal became to go completely against the grain; to change the story but keep all the visuals. And, having decided to change the story, we'd write dialogue to fit the story that you could fit into peoples' lips because the better the dub, the funnier the material.

"We figured out what our story was and then we would watch a scene and figure out the new dialogue. Our new arc was that semen was backing up into the little brother's brain. The new story has our heroine needing to make money to pay for her little brother's operation, fearing he may get too excited and that his head will explode. That was me and Charles, wacked out.

"I had gotten into the Writers Guild early and I was afraid that a couple of things would interfere, so I took the Creative Consultant title." Weisman would also be listed as the same on *Godzilla 1985: The Legend is Reborn* (1984), which explains some of the inappropriately funny things characters say to one another in the film's English-dubbed Japanese section and shoe-horned American sequences.

In regard to the voices for *Ferocious Female Freedom Fighters*, Charles Kaufman remembers, "I was kind of pals with Joey Gaynor, a very funny guy, and thought immediately that he would do the voices. Straw did some, too."

None of the voice talent names appear on the release of *Ferocious Female Freedom Fighters*. Throughout the years, it's filtered out that the L.A. Connection dubbed the film[10] with little details of which members of the troupe participated.

"Yeah, that was Bob Buchholz," says Kent Skov. "I don't know who else was with him, maybe Connie Sue Cook. I didn't know it was happening at first. The filmmakers didn't want to go to me because they wanted to get my cheap talent. I was making bigger deals so they kind of went around me and got Bob. I didn't make a big deal out of it. I said, 'Listen, if you guys can go out and make some money, go ahead and make some money.' It wasn't really cutting into our business. It's hard to tell people not to make money if they can. I don't think they got paid very much and the film never went anywhere that I know of."

Lloyd Kauffman says, "When the producer of this movie came to New York and saw the farting and the Elvis impersonator and the Jewish mother in a movie he had made as a serious kickboxing action film, he was, to say the least, overcome with great emotion and told us that if, by chance, the actors from Indonesia ever came to New York and saw the *Ferocious Female Freedom Fighters* we had created, they would kill us. Literally, we would be dead. We would be very dead."[11]

Troma opted out of doing a comedic redub of *Ferocious Female Freedom Fighters 2* (1982), which was a sequel in name only. The original film, *Membakar Matahari* (*To Burn the Sun*, 1983) may have come out a year prior to *Perempuan Bergairah*.[12] The company once again "Tromatized" a film twenty years later with the Belgian *Parts of the Family*, which utilized redubbing, as well as some newly shot scenes to make the 2003 Léon Paul De Bruyn version a palatable experience.

What's Up, Hideous Sun Demon?

There is a dearth of information about Craig Mitchell's *What's Up, Hideous Sun Demon?* (1983). Mitchell is also listed as a co-writer along with Allen and Mark Estrin (*Bare Essentials*, 1991). The film begins with a framing story with a bunch of rowdy college-aged boys grabbing some gross food and sitting down to watch the film. The sequence is notable only for the appearance of a young Mark Holton, who gained infamy as Francis Buxton in *Pee Wee's Big Adventure* (1985).

Director Craig Mitchell came to the project after it had already begun. "I don't know if it was producer Greg Brown's idea to do a *What's Up, Tiger Lily*-type redub movie, or if it was Allen and Mark Estrin who were involved in an earlier version of *What's Up, Hideous Sun Demon?* I believe they were all just young filmmakers who wanted to make a feature, and this was a way to get a movie produced inexpensively.

"I guess Greg wasn't satisfied with the earlier version, and he asked me to supervise a second pass. I cast Jay Leno and Susan Tyrrell. I suspect Leno wasn't sure what he was getting himself in for, so he didn't want his name used in promoting the film, or in the credits. I was never sure what was up with that.

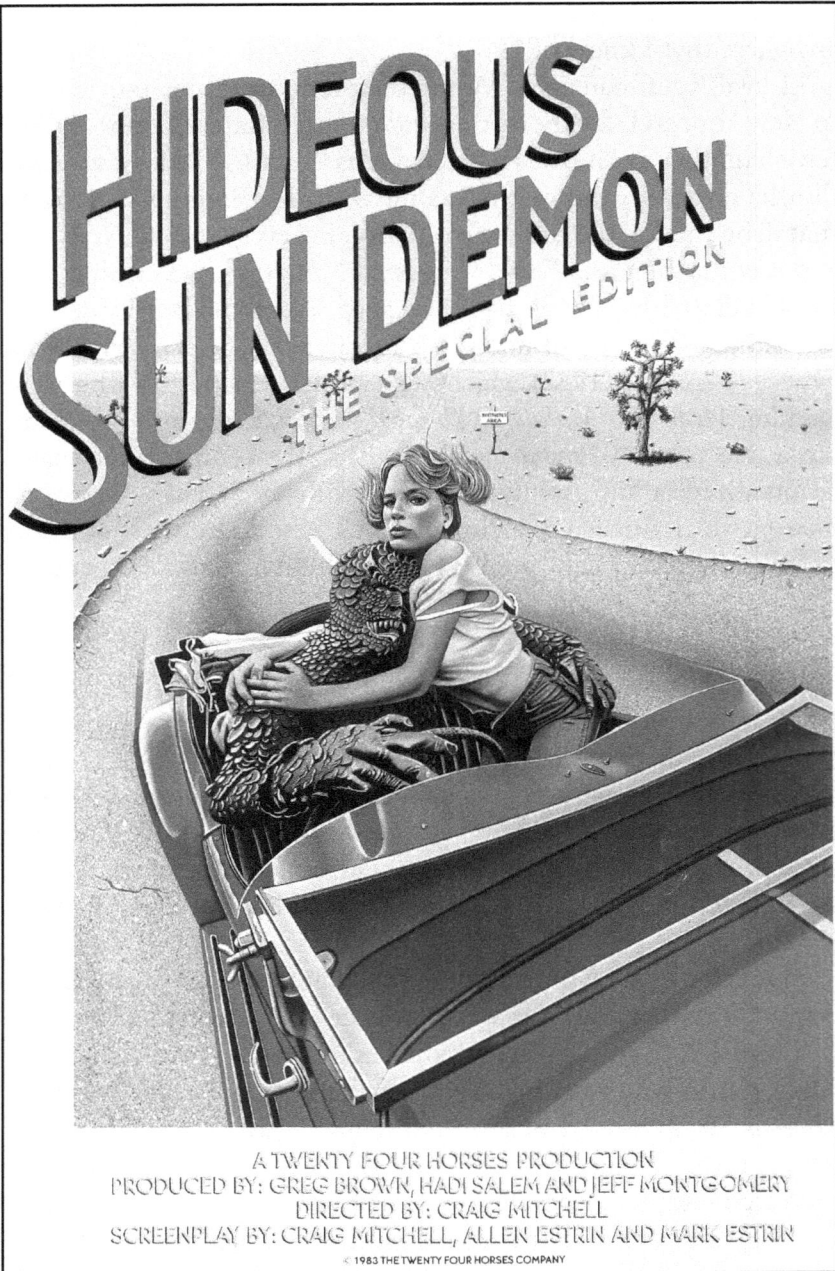

Alternate poster for *What's Up, Hideous Sun Demon?*

"I worked with a few joke writers, and one particular Additional Dialogue Recorder director, Richard Stern, who contributed a lot to the script. He had been dubbing Mexican soap operas into English so he knew a lot of good voice actors who filled in the minor parts, and Richard helped out with syncing and performance."

Voice actress Barbara Goodson recalls, "I worked for Jim Terry Productions and also his right hand man, Angelo Grillo. Jim was one of the first to bring in dubbing projects (mostly foreign) to L.A. in the '80s. Maybe even earlier.

"Jay Leno played [voiced] the lead and I voiced his girlfriend. We never worked at the same time. He was pretty well-known as a stand-up comic by then. Cam Clarke's father, Robert Clarke, was the original actor and I think Cam dubbed a role in it, as well."

Oddly, neither Goodson nor Mitchell knew if the film had ever been released. It came out on DVD—with Leno's name omitted—as *Revenge of the Sun Demon* (2003).

In 1982, Carl Reiner and Steve Martin, along with co-writer George Gipe, experimented in re-contextualization by placing Martin in *Dead Men Don't Wear Plaid* (1982) with a narrative that played against over a dozen Film Noir classics from 1941-1950. Reiner's film proved a major influence on other works that utilized existing footage to tell new stories via editing.

The L.A. Connection's TV show, *Mad Movies with the L.A. Connection*, played in syndication in late night slots around the country from 1985-86. It would be picked up later for *Nick at Nite* (1989-1991) and become one of the network's top shows. Meanwhile, the U.S.A Network show, *Night Flight*, which had often shown *J-Men Forever* in its eclectic four hour format, included six episodes of a Japanese TV series *Kagaku Sentai Dynaman* re-dubbed as *Dynaman*. One of a long tradition of multi-colored costumed monster-fighting squads, the five heroes of *Dynaman* faced-off against the treacherous Bernie Tanaka and Mel Fujitsu in adventures with such catchy titles as "The Lizard of Oz," "Lucky Pierre," and "Spunky the Wonder Squid."

Night of the Day

The early 1990s proved a heyday of "mock dub" films. The L.A. Connection's *Blobermouth* (1991) kicked off the decade along with David Casci's *A Man Called…Rainbo* (1990) and James Riffel's *Night of the Day of the Dawn of the Son of the Bride of the Return of the Revenge of the Terror of the Attack of the Evil, Mutant, Alien, Flesh Eating, Hellbound, Zombified Living Dead Part 2: In Shocking 2-D* (1991).

Casci's film took snippets of Robert Allen Schnitzer film *No Place to Hide* (1970) (AKA *Rebel*) which starred a young Sylvester Stallone. Casci surrounded the original bits with newly shot footage, integrating the two into a plot that plays off of Stallone's Rambo character.

Meanwhile, with *Night of the Day*, Riffel, using the name Lowell Mason, also incorporated some new footage, albeit far less than *A Man Called...Rainbo*, with his redub of George A. Romero's *Night of the Living Dead* (1968). It's more of a traditional mock dub that includes a running gag about a duck and a plot where the United States is divided into groups of over-worked zombies ". . . who are gathering their forces to crush and devour the other section, the Normals, the people who have managed somehow not to crack under the pressure." It's more akin to the haves and have-nots retelling of Kuang-chi Tu's *Tang shou tai quan dao* (*Crush*) for *Can Dialectics Break Bricks* (1972) than the L.A. Connection's reworking of the same source material for their *Mad Movies with the L.A. Connection* TV show.

Though *Night of the Day* has a "Part 2" subtitle, it's actually the first in a four-part series. What some consider the "lost" first part was a collection of shorts that James Riffel made while at New York University, including one called *Dead Dudes in The House* (1989). Riffel says, "When I walked into video stores at the time there was always an endless glut of horror films, including mine, and so I just thought up the most ridiculous title I could think of. As a joke, I ended up listing the forty-five-word title in *Variety*'s 'Films in Production' section. It immediately received major publicity solely based on the title. Radio DJs were talking about it, it appeared in the *New York Times* film section, it was mentioned on MTV, and someone even told me that Johnny Carson mentioned it on *The Tonight Show*.

"Back in the 1980s, editing space and film-to-tape transfers were very expensive, unlike today. So, I put the first version aside and used George Romero's *Night of the Living Dead*. I did this because his film was in the public domain, it was incredibly well-known, and I could make the 'film' for basically nothing. I made the original version in

1991 and distributed it myself through Palmer Video – a chain of roughly one hundred video stores based in New Jersey – and other 'mom and pop' shops across the U.S. I made 500 copies.

"The amazing part to me is that over a decade after its release, through no marketing, promotion, or pushing on my end, the film began to circulate on its own. People were making copies of copies and passing them around to friends. In the early 2000s, I started seeing copies on eBay going for $50-$100.

"The only other distribution it had was a theatrical release in New York in 2005. I had written and directed a feature film, *Mass of Angels* (2004), which was financed by the owner of a pharmaceutical company. He had actually heard of *Night of the Day* and wanted to see it. He became such a fan of the film that he rented a theater in New York City, The Two Boots Pioneer Theater, for a three-month theatrical run. This was a strange experience for me because I went to see the film a few times, and it was always packed, and people would say lines of dialogue like *The Rocky Horror Picture Show* (1975). A professor from NYU took an entire class to see the film. Someone from the *New York Times* called it 'a cult masterpiece.'"

Hercules Returns

The 1990s also brought to the fore some prime examples of dubbing from Australia. The cult television program, *The Aunty Jack Show*[13] (1972-1973) and its sketches "Gidget Goes Tasmanian" and "Herco the Magnificent,"[14] (mock dubs of *Blackbeard the Pirate* and a Hercules film respectively), influenced comedy groups Double Take and The Late Show. *The Late Show* television program ran from July 1992 until October 1993. During that time, it boasted two mock dub serials along with their skits, stand-up, street interviews, and more. The first, *The Olden Days,* dubbed the historical drama *Rush.* The new version mercilessly mocked the character Governor Frontbottom and contained a bonanza of facial hair jokes. The second season of *The Late Show* included a new take on the 1970s show *Bluey* as *Bargearse,* about a gruff, flatulent cop.

Double Take had been performing since 1986, doing live dubbing of films, such as *The Astro-Zombies* (1968), *The Phantom Empire* (1935), *Dance Hall Racket* (1953),[15] and *The Bees* (1978).[16] In 1989, the group began performing *Hercules Returns* (1993). Giorgio Capitani's

Samson and His Mighty Challenge AKA *Ercole, Sansone, Maciste e Ursus gli invincibili* (1964) was initially sent to Des Mangan via a friend. "As it is in Italian, he has no idea what the 1964 sword-and-sandal epic is really about."[12] This bit of real life would become a crucial plot point in *Hercules Returns*.

Producer Phil Jaroslow was struck by the audience reaction to the live version of Double Take Meet Hercules. Jaraslow, an American-born Melbournite, watched the end credits and began his search for the owner of the film rights. He also acquired Mangan's script before hiring Cinematographer and filmmaker David Parker to help write a story to wrap around Double Take's routine.[17]

Parker recalls, "I'd seen Double Take and had always been very amused and in awe of what they did. I think Des Mangan is a very clever fellow just to come up with the concept. I know it's been done in different forms in different parts of the world, but I don't think anyone did what Des did, which was basically take over a theater and use the concept of re-voicing a film live, which is what they did. So I got involved in this idea of doing a film based on that concept. Des came up with the idea of having a guy who was unhappy with his lot, working for a big distribution company so he takes over his own theater. On opening night, he finds his film's in Italian and not in English. So then you can swing into the idea that he has to rework it on the run. We had to ascertain how much of the success of Double Take was due to do with the tactility of the live performance, or could that idea be transferred into film."[18]

The wraparound stars David Argue as Brad McBane, a film purist working at a soulless distribution company. After a colorful exit, David renovates an old movie palace with the help of his projectionist, Sprocket (Bruce Spence) and spitfire publicist, Lisa (Mary Coustas). The trio "live dubs" the film in the projection booth while David's old boss (Michael Carman) stews in the audience. Ironically, Argue and Coustas are dubbed during the "live dubbing" scenes by Des Mangan and Sally Patience.

The film had its American premiere on January 28, 1993 at the Sundance Film Festival. The program didn't exaggerate when it said, "David Parker makes his debut with this film, and he hits the high-camp bull's-eye with each shot. Hercules is a delicious dingbat of a guy, and you'll laugh at him all the way."[19] Double Take continued live dubbing films for over a decade after *Hercules Returns*.

In 2003, another group toured the East Coast of Australia doing live dubbings of the 1981 Filipino spy movie *The Impossible Kid of Kung-fu,* which starred diminutive actor Weng Weng. Andrew Leavold worked with various cohorts, mostly the stars of his 2003 *Lesbo-A-Go-Go*; Eileen Surepuss, Fred Negro, and Pauline Bell. One notable performance at the Woodford Film Festival in Queensland found Leavold and Bell in a " . . . circus tent filled with ferals, stoners, yippies, yuppies, and the politically correct. Pauline and I practically threw away the literal translation on our script and cracked midget jokes for ninety minutes."

For years, cineastes reveled in another Australian export to the film world, the top notch Special Broadcasting Service TV subtitles were the de facto source for English translations of edgier world cinema. In the early 1990s, subtitlers Mary Pipes and Peter Templeton created a series of segments originally for private use but proved so popular the network allowed them to air. These are collectively known as *Revenge of the Subtitle* and share much with both Viénet's *Girls of Kamare* in the way the clips recontextualize on-screen action, providing completely new narratives that fit with a scene (or song, in the case of a Bollywood clip). Some of the fun comes from transliterating the clips based on similarities between words and phrases (¿Por qué?" becomes "Porky?").

The Mock Dub Heard 'Round the World

Meanwhile in France, Warner Bros. gave the film and television studio Canal+ Group carte blanche to their library. Michel Hazanavicius (*The Artist,* 2011) and Dominique Mézerette (*Dead Weight,* 2012) created collage works, *Ca détourne, Derrick contre Superman* (1992) and *La Classe américaine* (1992) (*Le Grand Détournement,* 1993) in the Situationist style.

Not to be outdone by the Aussies and the French, Kim Fuller and Geoff Atkinson of Spitting Image produced a series of mock dub shows, such as *The Staggering Stories of Ferdinand De Bargos* (1989), *Pallas* (1991), *The Almost Complete History of the 20th Century* (1993), *Klinik!* (1997), *Badly Dubbed Porn* (2005) and *Mashup Movie* (2009). These pay more heed to randy humor than to accurate lip synching.

The high point of the mock dub, which began with the L.A. Connection's *Blobermouth* in 1990, ended with the L.A. Connection's *Movie Madness Mystery* on the A&E network (1994). A few attempts to keep this style of comedy alive came from L.A. Connection alumni Bob Buchholz and Jeff Nimoy with TV shows, such as *Chimp Lip Theater* (1997) and *Gotcha* (1998).

Picking up the mantle, the Jet City Improv group of Seattle, Washington has been performing *Twisted Flicks* occasionally since 1997. They've live-dubbed such films as *The Son of Kong* (1933), *Creature from the Black Lagoon* (1954), *Santa Claus Conquers the Martians (1964), The Abominable Snowman* (1957), and *The Face of Fu Manchu* (1965).[20]

The Peanut Gallery

It's no coincidence that the abatement in dubbing would coincide with the rise in popularity of a similar concept, "riffing," exemplified by *Mystery Science Theater 3000* (1988-1999). Akin to what some movie hosts had been doing (most notably Rich Koz's Svengoolie), *Mystery Science Theater 3000* added its characters into the films they lampooned via an inexpensive video effect that displayed their silhouettes as sitting in the front row of a theater in which they and the audience sat. The hosts mocked (not mock dubbed) the films, putting the viewers in collusion with the show. More than just discussing the films and their possible shortcomings, the hosts of *Mystery Science Theater 3000* also made myriad clever references to popular and classical culture.

Some attribute the success of *Mystery Science Theater 3000* to the home-taping and tape trading of fans. As the adoption of VCRs had reached a saturation point by the late 1980s, fans could capture and share what had before been ephemeral. The producers of *Mystery Science Theater 3000* would remind viewers to "keep circulating the tapes" in the credits of the show.

After the cancellation of *Mystery Science Theater 3000*, the cast split into new comedy groups, such as Rifftrax, The Film Crew, and Cinematic Titanic. While Cinematic Titanic (2007-2013) and The Film Crew (2004-2008) riffed public domain films, Rifftrax (2004-Present) got around the public domain issue by providing stand-alone audio tracks that could be synched at home to any DVD release. Obviously, technology has changed the way in which films are delivered—both at home and in theaters—and also the nature of the presentations themselves.

In 2000, Neil Cicierega began creating a series of "animutations," such as *Hyakugojyuuichi!!!*, wherein Japanese lyrics were "transliterated" into Dadaist English subtitles. Also in the same year, the short film, *Mondo Ford* (2000), provided laughs by combining historical photographs, an Italian language tutorial, and English subtitles to create a "documentary." Presented as a lost film by "Ricardo Fratteli" (AKA Scott Calonico), *Mondo Ford* tells a wild story of a vast conspiracy involving aliens and Gerald Ford.

Mash-Ups and Beyond

Both of the aforementioned works found their greatest audience via the quickly evolving Internet, which provided a platform for distribution as tools for the creation and manipulation of materials became more affordable. This led to the evolution of the "mash-up," the combining of existing materials into new forms. Mash-ups had their roots in collages, found footage films, such as Bruce Connor's *A Movie* or Craig Baldwin's *Tribulation 99: Alien Anomalies under America*; and cut-in albums, such as Dickie Goodman's *Mr. Jaws*). Musically, The Kleptones exemplified this style with their album *A Night at the Hip-Hopera*, which blended Queen and several other artists. Visually, mash-ups included videos, such as the *Gymkata* Mentos commercial or the rx mix of George Bush singing U2's "Sunday Bloody Sunday."

In 1996, an episode of *Star Trek: Deep Space Nine* used footage from the original *Star Trek* series, placing contemporary characters into the prior episode. Similarly, comedian Steve Oedekerk embraced technology to remove the main character from actor/director "Jimmy" Wang Yu's *Hu hao shuang xing* (1976) (AKA *The Savage Killers* or *Tiger and Crane Fist*), placing himself into the action. Oedekerk also shot a great deal of original footage, badly dubbing both the new and old. The result, *Kung Pow: Enter the Fist* (2002), was consistently savaged by critics upon release.

Jonathan Foreman of the *New York Post* called the film ". . . an inept, tedious spoof of '70s kung-fu picture that contains almost enough chuckles for a three-minute sketch, and no more."[21] Eddie

Cockrell at *Variety* described the film as an "...unwatchable embarrassment," although he did correctly predict that the "...consistently silly and intermittently laugh-out-loud funny spoof will be consigned primarily to genre fans."[22] Indeed, the film has found a limited and faithful audience over the years.

Though an accomplished writer, producer, and director, Oedekerk may have been best-known at the time for his "Thumbmation," where he added facial features and goofy voices to thumbs, parodying popular films such as *Star Wars*, *The Godfather*, and *The Blair Witch Project*. Oedekerk utilized this in *Kung Pow: Enter the Fist* with the recurring joke of having a face on his character's tongue. It's a technique that would later be copied by Dane Boedigheimer for the Annoying Orange web character. The tongue gag and a poorly animated fight with a cow may not be successful, but *Kung Pow: Enter the Fist* still works as an interesting experiment in the editing and integration of extant and new footage.

Since the release of *Kung Pow: Enter the Fist*, there has been a dearth of mainstream mock dubs released theatrically. All forms of the mock dub, redubbed dialogue, *détourned* subtitles, and riffing, could be found on the Internet, where the supposed democratization of content allowed anyone to create video or audio projects.

From their days at inner-city grindhouse theaters, kung-fu films have played a role in hip hop culture. The Shaw Brothers film *Duel of the Iron Fist* (1971) (*Da jue dou*) was the basis for Peter Bavaro's *Iron Fist Pillage* (2001) starring Cappadonna (*née* Darryl Hill) of the Wu-Tang Clan. The same aesthetic of hip hop and kung-fu fueled the web series, *Kung Faux* (2003-2007), where artists such as De La Soul and Queen Latifah loosely dubbed visually stylized clips from classic chopsocky flicks, peppering the proceedings with a "gangsta" patois and endless "chronic" references.

The popular Spike TV show, *Most Extreme Elimination Challenge* (2003-2007), took an already funny show, *Takeshi's Castle* (1986-1990), and included a new soundtrack of bad puns and sexual double entendres. Removing the comedy, the show was recreated as *Wipeout* for ABC in 2011.

On the more political end of the mock dub spectrum, neo-Situationist works like Doug Miles's *Don't Ask, Don't Tell*, which discussed gays in the military and the political climate of 2002 via dubbing W.

Lee Wilder's *Killer's from Space.* The Stolen Collective's *The Lord of the Rings: The Fellowship of the Ring of Free Trade* (2002) and *The Lord of the Rings: The Twin Towers* (2004) rework Peter Jackson's films as treatises on the World Trade Organization via editing and new subtitles. Similarly, *Guerre des étoiles existentielles* (*Existential Star Wars*) (2001) takes a French dub of George Lucas's film and "translates" it back via subtitles that paint a very bleak, Sartre-esque picture.

In 2005, James Riffel released two more entries in his *Night of the Day of the Dawn of the Son of the Bride of the Return of the Revenge of the Terror of the Attack of the Evil, Mutant, Alien, Flesh Eating, Hellbound, Zombified Living Dead* series. Both were made for less than $100 in answer to the inflated budgets of Steven Spielberg's *War of the Worlds* (2005) and Peter Jackson's *King Kong* (2005). Riffel provided another entry in 2011 with a shorter work that updated classic television shows with more ribald modern dialogue to exemplify the digression of mores in popular culture.

Something much closer to the L.A. Connection's recent style of mock dubbing is the series of YouTube videos by Bad Lip Reading. Begun in 2011, the source behind Bad Lip Reading remains anonymous.[23] Taking on everything from music videos to film scenes to politicians, the new words dubbed into these bits of pop culture effluvia are surreal translates along the lines of Rebecca Black singing "Gang fight, gang fight, have I brought enough chicken for us to thaw?" to the refrain of the song "Friday."

The potential illegalities of these works that play fast and loose with intellectual property (some are protected parodies, others are closer to theft), coupled with the ephemeral nature of the Internet often makes for a "blink and you'll miss it" bit of entertainment rather than a cultural artifact. Likewise, as copyright laws morph and copyright holders are bought out and/or transferred, many of the works mentioned here run the risk of being ensnared by legalities or laziness, only to become lost works.

The L.A. Connection.

Reefer Madness II: The True Story

During their run on "Thicke of the Night," the L.A. Connection began putting a new spin on the 1936 drug scare film, *Reefer Madness*. "With the help of the L.A. Connection comedy troupe, a California group has acquired worldwide distribution rights and plans to re-issue the camp classic with a fictitious, dubbed sound track . . . The new movie, expected out sometime within the year, will be called *Reefer Madness: The True Story*."[24]

"The movie was born after we presented a live three-part version of *Cat-Women of the Moon* to the American Film Institute," remembers Skov. "We did twenty minutes each day to the same group. It was a seminar over the weekend type of deal, and there were a couple of hundred—maybe 250 people. Afterward, a couple of the attendees talked about doing a deal with them. One of them, Randall Nogg, had more money than the other and he seemed pretty excited, so we made a deal."

Nogg recalls, "I had been out in L.A. a little over a year and hadn't been getting terribly far with getting where I wanted. Part of that was that the economy was just terrible; there wasn't a lot of production going on. As I was sitting in the auditorium, there was a guy next to me dressed very nicely in a suit and tie, which seemed unusual compared to us Hollywood-types, who were all in our jeans. But, he was laughing along with the rest of us and seemed to really enjoy what the L.A. Connection was doing. Turns out he was the next speaker and he was some fairly high-up person at 20th Century Fox. It got me thinking, *Here's somebody who saw what they were doing and really seemed to like it*. I started putting things together in my mind. If I could get people at a studio laughing like that, that's a good sign. I was aware of *What's Up, Tiger Lily?* and thought that this would be a way to make a film relatively inexpensively. Based on this guy's reaction, maybe I could get some interest."

Skov says, "Nogg wanted to know what movie I thought would be the biggest seller out of the ones we had done before. We've done maybe twenty-five movies total over the years, but at that time, had done only about six or eight and most of the movies we had done were not officially in the public domain. I know *Attack of the 50 Foot Woman* was one, *Wrestling Women Versus the Aztec Mummy, Plan 9 from Outer Space, Cat-Women* of course, *Sex Madness,* and *Reefer Madness.*"

Nogg continues, "Over the next month or so I got the money together and started to negotiate with Kent and his people. I had an option with them for maybe two months where it was all contingent on getting a movie. Kent had given me a list and I wanted to find out if I could buy rights for any of these movies.

"Quite frankly, of all the movies they had done that I had seen, *Plan 9 from Outer Space* was the one I was strongest on. It had the reputation of being the worst movie ever made but, more than that, it worked really well with what they already had as a script. I began a search to see who owned *Plan 9 from Outer Space* and I found out a hell of a lot more about old movies than I really wanted to know."

The director of *Plan 9 from Outer Space*, Edward D. Wood Jr., had passed away in 1978. Nogg couldn't determine if the film had gone into the public domain or not. Eventually, he learned of film collector Wade Williams, who claimed that he bought the rights to *Plan 9 from Outer Space* from Wood's widow. "It seemed like he had the inside track to ownership of this," says Nogg.

Just as soon as things were moving forward, the brakes were applied when another person claimed that they owned the rights to *Plan 9 from Outer Space*. "He was very shady," says Nogg. "He didn't have a very good reputation. He claimed that he purchased the rights from a television syndicator in L.A. who had purchased them from Ed Wood Jr. It all seemed a little far-fetched. He only had a 16mm print while Wade Williams had a 35mm." Nogg tried to put his lawyers in touch with this second "rights-holder," to no avail. Rather than opening himself up for a future lawsuit, Nogg opted to walk away from *Plan 9 from Outer Space* and scrambled to find a new title to lock in with the L.A. Connection.

Nogg began looking into the other films that the L.A. Connection had dubbed. However, the studios that owned the rights weren't willing to talk to him about such a small project. Finally, Nogg began investigating *Reefer Madness,* which was indeed in the public domain. From there, he began searching for a complete print and/or negative of the film. He even went to the Library of Congress, who claimed to have had the negative but couldn't find it when pressed. Fortunately, Wade Williams had a complete 35mm print of *Reefer Madness*.

With this project, Murphy's Law was fully enacted: Everything that can go wrong will go wrong. Moreover, something called "Randy's Law" came into play: Everything that can't go wrong will go wrong, too.

"First thing, we got the film and I had to transfer it all to video," says Nogg. He quickly found out that the one reel he had checked for quality had been the best reel. The rest of the film was a bit more beaten up and some scenes were missing, including the film's prologue. "Some of it was just faded so badly; I mean, you could see it but it just wasn't so great." That's how it started and it all went downhill from that point.

Nogg had several meetings with Skov and the nine other writers on the project. "I said, 'Look, you guys are very funny and what you do in the theaters is very funny, but we can't just take the script that you use in the theater because what you do there is a different process with an audience than it will be when it's not live. The expectations are different.' And they were like, 'Yeah, yeah, yeah, we understand, no problem.' A few weeks later, I looked at the first draft with my partner, Herb Golden, and found that it was the same thing they did in the theaters. It wasn't going to work.

"I sat back down with them and re-explained myself. I don't know how many revisions we went through—at least half a dozen—before they finally seemed to catch on to what we needed. They just seemed mentally locked in to what they had been doing for a live show and were not comprehending why that wouldn't work for what we were doing.

"We started doing read-throughs over at Kent's house. He had assigned roles based on what they had done before. They had their scripts in hand and we would sit there in front of the TV and act it out over the next hour and a half, taking notes on what was working and what wasn't working."

Skov adds, "What we did is that we broke it up into segments and then I oversaw the segments to make sure they were all tied together. What I was doing back then was creating a writers group that wasn't just doing movie dubbing but also sketches. I had a group of about ten people.

"I always wanted to be fair and incorporate as many of the people that were working for me for free so when we got *Reefer Madness II* I wanted to incorporate them into the project. Some wrote more than others; some were more effective than others. Ultimately we got the script that we had which I thought was a pretty good script at the time. I wouldn't call it our best work because it was one of the first things that we did in terms of putting together something to sell."

Bob Buchholz adds, "Ten writers was certainly more than we needed and made it a much more difficult process than it needed to be because you try to get ten people to agree on anything and it doesn't really work. I think we learned from it, though, because when we got to the series we knew that we couldn't have that many people— not that there was a budget to pay that many writers. But, we didn't know any better at the time; we were just learning. We didn't even have an office; we were working out of Kent's home. It was really a tight-budgeted thing and we did it when we could."

Writer John McCann says, "It was fairly chaotic. It felt like we spent an awful lot of time watching the movie and drinking."

"It was a fairly lengthy process," says Nogg. "Once we finally got a script that we could live with, we got a recording studio set up." Nogg hired a fellow Nebraskan to help locate a studio and arrange an audio engineer. "At the time, nobody had video in their audio studios, so we had to arrange to bring in what was then 'state of the art' equipment, bringing in a projection TV.

"We went in and went over and over it until we got it sounding the way we wanted. Again, we kept running into things. I don't know if it was an entire day but it was damn near close to an entire day where nothing we recorded actually hit the tape. One of the assistants from the studio apparently didn't know how to hit 'RECORD' properly. It wasn't like the studio said, 'Oh, we're really sorry, we'll give you two extra days,' or something. No, they just said, 'These things happen.' That should have been my warning about them.

"We got it to a point where we thought we had what we were looking for. We were ready to marry it to the video tape and take a look. I go to pick up the two-inch audio tapes before I take them over to the lab and, when I get there, they say, 'Here's the bill.' It was probably a good $10,000 more than it should have been. They had tacked on a charge for rental of the TV after telling me that it would be part of the daily rate. We went back and forth on that. I eventually realized that I had been naïve enough to trust the wrong person. It came down to either paying for the tapes or walking away and starting over. Had I known then what I know now, I would have walked away.

"I ended up paying for it, and when we went back to look at it … it was okay but it still wasn't quite working the way that we needed it to. The recording sounded too good. The voices were way too up front and not at all like they would have sounded in the movie. No, you're not going to match it word for word but the sound wasn't working properly. Needless to say, I wasn't going to go back to that first studio so I had to find another one.

"We started over and did it all over again; another two weeks of recording. This time, I think we were closer but the sound still wasn't quite right and some of the jokes were falling flat. By the time we lined it up to go back to the studio, they had closed."

The third time wasn't the charm, but it worked.

Then it became time to shoot a new prologue for the film. Running at just 66:00, Nogg needed at least four more minutes for *Reefer Madness II* to qualify as a feature-length film.

"The prologue that you see on the film is not the first one we shot, or even the second, or third, or fourth one. The first idea was a spoof of the old *Mission: Impossible* TV show, where Kent would be the Jim Phelps character and he had to re-dub the movie to tell the 'true story' of the film. To keep our budget low, we were going to shoot it all silently and do everything in a voice-over. We'd see Kent walking in while wearing a trench coat – with nothing on underneath – listening to the recording, and going through this file folder full of pictures where he finds a picture of the L.A. Connection sitting around an Edsel. That's where the photos at the end of *Reefer Madness II* come from.

"Even though we shot the whole thing, it just didn't work. Nobody seemed to really like it. It just sat there and it didn't really explain the story very well. So, I went to the L.A. Connection and said, 'You guys come up with something. Come up with a five to seven minutes prologue that's going to set up the story.' But, for some reason, they never seemed to come up with anything. By this time, we had been working on this for so long that a few of the original people—at least two or three of them—had quit the company. I asked one of the guys who had left, John McCann, if he could come up with anything.

"He came up with this kind of *60 Minutes* spoof, where an investigative reporter tracks down the original Jack Perry character. It was very funny; off the wall, goofy, crazy. Kent rejected it out of hand. He wouldn't deny that he rejected it but he might deny the reason that he did; because they did not part on good terms and Kent was not about to let McCann have any part of this. But, they couldn't come up with anything else.

John McCann adds, "I wrote a few of them. There was one called 'Time Bomb,' where there was a time bomb in the theater and the critic had to finish his review by a certain time or the bomb would go off."

Nogg continues, "Finally, I sat down and I came up with the idea of spoofing Siskel & Ebert. What I ended up writing was too long but I was trying to get everything and the kitchen sink in, in terms of explaining what people were seeing. We were running out of time, so Kent grudgingly okayed it. It wasn't the funniest or the best, but it would work. Out of desperation, we proceeded with that one.

"We cast it with two guys from the L.A. Connection that we could agree on; Sandy Mielke and Scott Weintraub. I went back out to raise more money to shoot it because that was going to be shot on 35mm. I rented the location and found a really nice guy who had his own 35mm camera. He had a bunch of friends who were young filmmakers. They all were volunteering except the lighting guy, who I shouldn't have paid because I could have done a better job. The only thing I couldn't find was a sound guy who I could afford. I could rent the gear without the guy or the guy without the gear. So, I ran the sound myself. Running the sound on the project divided my attention too much.

"Now, Kent is a very creative guy, but he really had no experience in film at that time. He knew a little about TV from *Thicke of the Night* but not about film. I sat down with Kent the night before our shoot and I told him that this had to go smoothly. We had one day and had to get this right.

"Now, in terms of credit, Kent is the Director. Even though he doesn't know what he's doing, he's directing this. I mean, he can direct people, but in terms of the technical aspects—which, on a film, is half or more of what a director has to do. We sat for maybe two hours and I took him step by step. 'Here's the process, here's what's going to happen, here's what you say, here's what we do.' I told him, 'Look, I'll set up most of the shots; you don't have to worry about it. When the time comes, you just say 'Action' and 'Cut.'

"We get to the shooting and Kent is spending most of his time with the two actors. That's fine. That's his strong suit anyway. By the time we got started we were already two hours behind with the lighting and having to remove seats from the screening room. I wanted to keep things as simple as possible so there were really only five basic shots for the whole shoot; the establishing shot, then we had two close-up shots, a reverse shot of the character of Jack in silhouette, and then we had what were the most critical shots, what were in effect over-the-shoulder shots. Those would be critical for cutting back and forth.

"We proceed, time ticking away, and get to the over-the-shoulder shots. I realize that we're just not going to have enough time here so I need to figure out a way to convince the guy who runs the screening room we rented to give me a little more time without charging us more money. I could tell that he was already a little irritated because we had to remove some of the seats. I worked with the cameraman to get the one over-the-shoulder shot set and then said, 'Okay, I've got to go talk to talk to this guy and see what we can do to stay.'

"Initially, the guy didn't want to give us any more time. 'You paid to be here until five o'clock and that's all the time you're getting.' I had to plead with him, telling him that we were a low budget production. Even though he saw some of the problems we were having, he still thought that we were some kind of bigger production and had all the money in the world. He didn't believe me when I told him that I was the Producer. 'But you're the guy running the sound and helping to pull the seats out of the theater.' Yes, I'm doing that and I'm producing the film. So, he suddenly softened up and let me have another hour for maybe another hundred bucks. I bought us some time.

"I go back in, feeling pretty good, and we shot the one over-the-shoulder and I tell the cameraman to just match the same thing on the other side.

"Unbeknownst to me, while I was out talking to the screening room guy, Kent had taken it upon himself to check out the shot that we had set up. He told the cameraman, 'Oh, no, no, no, this has to be a real tight shot.' Basically, he took what was an over-the-shoulder shot and made it this extreme close-up. The actor's face filled the screen. When I came back, no one told me that Kent had changed the shot. And, of course, when I told the cameraman to match the shot, I just assumed it was the same as what I set up. Instead, we ended up with two useless shots. When I sat down to watch the footage when we got it back from the lab I remember shouting out, 'What the fuck is that?'

"Suddenly, the two main shots I have to cut away from the establishing shot are gone. I'm down from five shots down to three. I certainly don't have money to go back and shoot it again, so that's what we were stuck with. It turned into a huge nightmare. I was furious. I wouldn't even let Kent in on the editing session. I was livid.

"See, we had an agreement. Kent and I had a 50/50 say-so about the film and the creativity. You always need someone to have the final decision. Kent really wanted that prologue to be done very seriously; no laughs, not even tongue-in-cheek humor. That was another reason that it's not scripted to be as funny as it could be. And, as you're aware, compromise rarely works in creative situations.

"I put together the prologue into some semblance of the prologue, which ended up being too long; however, I couldn't cut away to anything to tighten things up. It wasn't terrible but it wasn't what it should have been. A few years later, I took another chop at it after watching it so many times, but it's still not ideal.

"When it came to distribution, I had been shopping it around even before it was finished. Back then, there were a lot more small distribution places. The reaction I got was strange: a lot of them really liked it but didn't want to take it. If you remember Orion distribution, they were a fairly big company at the time. I dropped off a copy to them at the end of the week and called the guy on Monday to see if he had had a chance to see it. He told me, 'Randy, I was so glad that you brought this in because we had been having just a horrible week but we screened this on Friday before we all went home and we all laughed hysterically and, really, it gave us a much better weekend because of it. I'm just so happy that you brought this in, but we're not interested.'

"That really made my head spin. The feeling was that *Reefer Madness II* was a small film, it would take a lot of word-of-mouth to advertise it, and it would take a while to grow and find an audience. That's not what they were interested in. They were already getting into that blockbuster mindset; release a film and have it make big box office that opening weekend. That's still a problem with the Hollywood model.

"I tried every company you can think of and the response was the same, when I got a response. I started going to second and third tier and, finally, I got one nibble on the line. I met with this company and they really rolled out the red carpet. We had this meeting. The president of the company was there. We were all sitting around this big conference table, the whole deal. However, I started getting this real used car salesman vibe from this. I took the contract back to my attorneys and had them look it over and the contract was terrible. It was one of these things where they just wanted to write off anything and everything on the film before they would ever show a profit; Hollywood accounting. The distributors get their money off the top and I'd never see a dime.

"My attorneys, though, were telling me that I should sign the contract just to get the film distributed. Maybe I'd make money on the second project. The problem was that all of the money I had raised for the project was from friends and family. I wouldn't feel right by just saying, 'Hey, I'll have a film that gets good exposure, so forget all of them.' In good conscience, I couldn't do that. I turned down the contract and it was a good thing I did because six months later, I read an article in *Variety* about the guy who ran the company—the one who gave me the creepiest vibe—running off with all the money, leaving everyone else high and dry. Another six months later, they had gone under.

"I kept searching and finally found Seymour Borde and Associates. They were a small distributor that had gotten their big break with *Kentucky Fried Movie*. They also did some harmless T&A exploitation stuff. Fine. They knew the business. The son, Mark Borde, ran the company, and he called me a few days after I dropped off the film, wanting to make a deal. They offered me a contract that wasn't terrible. Later on, I found out that Mark hadn't even screened the film. It was his secretary who watched it and talked him into it.

"We made the deal and, in the same idea that everything that could go wrong would. They ran the film in a test market. I had tested it before and knew it played well, so I didn't care. He lined it up in Seattle for a Sunday afternoon. Not the best time, but we were getting some free promotion from a local radio station, so that should help. But, that same Sunday was a playoff game between the Sea Hawks and the Raiders. We were going head to head against the playoffs. You would have thought someone in Seattle might have told us that this wasn't the best time. As it turned out, maybe a dozen people showed up in this theater that sat over 300.

"I didn't want to wait until Monday or Tuesday to talk to the distributor to find out how the screening went, so I had someone up there put me in touch with the projectionist. He told me about the football game and how few people were there. Of course, I was disappointed. However, he told me that even over the noise of the projector; he was able to hear the people in the audience laughing. I took that as the one positive out of this whole thing.

"I go into the distributor's office where they told me that no one had showed up, omitting the whole idea of the football game. Even after I brought that up, the distributor insisted that if we had a good movie that people would have come out. He just didn't get it. He had his mind made up. There was no way he was going to get an audience for it.

"He spent the next couple of months trying to pre-sell everything: the video rights, the TV rights, all of that, to get enough money to get it to play in the theaters. But, in particular, he was not able to get anyone interested in selling the video rights. That really surprised me as I had already talked to a few video distributors who seemed very interested before I even finished the project. But, everyone was turning it down. I did some investigation and found that the distributor was telling people that the film wasn't going to be released theatrically. Without that, the video folks were hesitant to put it out on video. Basically, the distributor was cutting his own throat and, by extension, mine. There was a logic that Mark was just missing.

"Finally, a year went by and it hadn't gone into theaters so I enacted the contractual clause to get the film back.

"I went through another round of trying to sell it to distributors before I finally gave up and decided to distribute it myself—a very foolish proposition. The only thing I knew about distribution was that most of the people doing it were crooks.

"I had the two prints of the film and managed to get them into Los Angeles, New York, Cleveland, Cincinnati, St. Louis, Austin, and Portland. Even though I explained to the theater people the limited appeal of the film, the most they would give us was a midnight show for just a few weeks. I was trying to convince them to give it months to let the word of mouth build up but none of them would let it run long enough. Plus, the theaters didn't want to pay for advertising. They wanted me to do that. I tried to do as much as I could with the money I had, like putting an ad in a local college paper.

"The best screening we had was in St. Louis, where it ran for about four weeks. The theater even admitted to me that the film was just starting to get some legs when they had to pull it because they already had contracts with other things that had to run. The worst screening was probably New York. I had it in a theater that wasn't far from New York University (NYU). The theater owner was really enthusiastic and encouraging. Yet, the opening weekend got his with a huge snowstorm and there was a shooting right between NYU and the theater. Basically, no one could get to the theater if they wanted to. Again, maybe a half dozen people showed up and the theater owner is furious. He calls me up on Monday morning and told me that I didn't do a good enough job advertising it! By mid-week, he decided he was going to pull it, even though we had a reviewer from *The Village Voice* coming in that Saturday to see it but, no, he got cold feet.

"I took it to the cable channels: the Comedy Channel, HA!, HBO. I even had a friend who worked at HBO and I managed to set up a screening with them on a Friday night. I did it up big, bringing in popcorn and all that. The screening went really well, but the guy in charge didn't show up—the decision-maker. For the next few weeks I talked to his secretary repeatedly before she finally told me to just go ahead and send it to New York, that the real decisions were made there. They turned it down flat.

"It got to the point where I just had to laugh. It was either cry or laugh. Had the movie been a piece of crap, I could have probably walked away and said, 'We tried.' But, I really thought we had done something good. And, what's more, it's held up after all these years. That's what frustrates me more than anything. People who see it generally seem to like it, but it just never got a chance to find an audience.

"After another year or two of not getting anywhere, I ended up putting it out on VHS and then DVD. I made the website www.reefermadness2.com, did a little marketing, and we sold a little bit, but not much. People don't tend to buy movies that they don't know much about. It probably costs me more to keep the website going than I make from the occasional sale.

"Kent and I still stay in touch a little bit. I got a call from him a few years ago when he wanted to do *Reefer Madness* again live. Legally, he couldn't do it without my permission since that could undercut my sales. I agreed, of course, and he did it live.

Skov adds, "We did it live for about two years at the Laemmle theater before moving it to our own theater. We perform *Reefer Madness* live now. We've updated some of the stuff but we've kept some of the stuff we did then. There's a lot of music that we couldn't use for the movie that we can use for live shows. For example, we use 'Everybody Must Get Stoned' by Bob Dylan for the opening song when we do it live."

Meanwhile, copies of the film are still available via Randy Nogg's site. He's still hoping that the film will get its due.

26 HALF-HOURS FOR FALL 1985

PUT
MAD MOVIES
ON YOUR
SCHEDULE

"Mad Movies" are films and television shows with all new comedy soundtracks, elaborately created with music and sound effects.

Each episode features a condensed film or television show; a candid "man on the street" interview sequence, an actual home movie or video (that audience members are welcomed to submit) and previews of coming attractions. Also, when possible, people involved in the original production of the episode's "mad movie" will be interviewed, with amusing results.

Put "Mad Movies" on your schedule and bring your audience the newest, most hysterical comedy concept.

IMPROVISION

"Mad Movies" are developed in a process called "Improvision" by the L.A. Connection, a Southern California-based comedy group.

They began developing the concept in 1982. Sitting in the front row of a movie theater with microphones and a synthesizer, they'd project a film (including such "camp classics" as "Plan 9 from Outer Space" and "Attack of the Fifty Foot Woman") without the sound and create a live comedy soundtrack on the spot.

Touring the state of California, the group packed theaters and pleased audiences with the "Improvision" technique.

Now Four Star brings "Improvision" to the television screen on a weekly basis with "Mad Movies with the L.A. Connection."

Advertisement for Mad Movies.

Mad Movies

Come on everybody, we're headed in a new direction.
Going down town with the L.A. Connection.
To see the ma-ma-ma-Mad Movies.

— Theme song to *Mad Movies with The L.A. Connection*

"Doing 'Flicke of the Night' really helped us get *Mad Movies with the L.A. Connection*," says Kent Skov. "We put together a demo reel of about seven minutes of clips from 'Flicke of the Night' and started shopping it around. A little while later, my neighbor had a friend over. The doors were open and you could hear them laughing and having a good time and we had a pretty friendly situation. So, I just kind of walked into their house and said, 'How're you doing?' My neighbor, Susan Lenti, introduced me to her boyfriend, Randy Ridges. He worked over at Gold Key Entertainment."

Randy Ridges remembers, "I went to see Kent's show, it was *Plan 9 from Outer Space*, I believe. I thought it was great. It was hilarious. The next time I saw him I told him what I was doing and that maybe we should talk to Gold Key's president and see if we could get ahold of some of the films in the Gold Key library. That was the whole genesis of the thing—transforming it from a live show to a TV series."

Kurt Gardner, the former Director of Promotions at Four Star International writes, "The Gold Key film library consisted of some of the cheesiest, most low-budget, drive-in theater crap you've never heard of: ultra-obscure foreign sci-fi, drive-in epics from Crown International and a few art films thrown in for good measure."

"Gold Key merged with Four Star, a super-cheesy syndicator of low-budget films like *Plan 9 from Outer Space* before it escalated into bad movie immortality. Four Star had been formed by stars Dick Powell, David Niven, Charles Boyer, and Ida Lupino in 1952, but by the time I arrived in 1984, the glimmer was all but gone," says Gardner.

As a production company, Four Star had been inactive since 1975. The plan was to revive the production arm with the new merger. "We became the first show they sold in a long time," says Skov. "They did *Four Star Theater* with Dick Powell and *Wanted: Dead or Alive* with Steve McQueen.

"We were a way for their company to get a brand and come back with a big splash. My point is that it was right place, right time. I mean, you have to have the skillset to pull it off. You just can't sell something if you can't do it, but you have to have some luck for things like this to continue to happen for you and that I have.

"Four Star had an even better library, and they had a guy named Dick Cignarelli. He was head of distribution for Four Star. He brought *The Benny Hill Show* into America, so he had somewhat of a good track record with unknown comedy getting on syndicated American television."

"We went to Ben Barry, formerly of Gold Key, and Dick Cignarelli and pitched the idea," says Ridges. "At the time, I was selling syndication for those guys and I was flying from L.A. to the Midwest and trying to sell these schlocky TV packages to television stations in Green Bay; really third-tier markets. It was a miserable existence. I was close to being shown the door by Cignarelli. Once we pitched the idea, I pretty much left the company to work with Kent on doing the TV show. Once I saw what Kent was doing with public domain films, it was obvious to me that he needed to get in and talk to Four Star about breathing new life into the film vault."

The first pilot pitched was called *Dungeon Women*. Skov describes it as, "Judy Landers tied up by her sister in a dungeon. She was shackled to the wall and forced to watch bad old movies. Those would be our movies. That was the concept. We had little wraparound funny things. We even had Jerry 'The Beaver' Mathers on that pilot as a guest star. Elvira was around at that time, so we were trying to do a little bit of that kind of fun campiness."

Kurt Gardner remembers the pilot as "an attempt to incorporate the then-current mud wrestling craze. It featured Audrey Landers as one of two scantily-dressed, breasty (*sic*) bimbos wrestling around on a dirt floor and introducing redubbed clips from terrible movies."[25]

Randy Ridges adds, "We filmed this at Kent Weishaus's mother's house. They had a basement, which is very unusual for houses in Southern California. We had those girls go up and down the cellar stairs a lot of times. That was the one time that we spent money and rented a soundstage and actually had a set design and everything else."

John McCann says, "I helped write the wraparounds for it. The bat on the string and all that cheesy stuff. I think Ken Segall and I worked on a lot of that."

Skov continues, "We took the pilot to KTLA. I was there with Cignarelli and meeting with the head of programming. He took a look at the show and told us, 'That's just too kinky; they're not going to buy that in the Midwest.' He thought we were nuts. He looked at me and said, 'Kent, you're a funny guy, why don't *you* host the show?' And I'm thinking, 'Me host the show? I don't know if all the writers are going to like this if I host the show,' because that put me in a different place than everyone else (even though I was already the director and producer)."

The troupe regrouped and stuck to the basics. The pilot for *Mad Movies with the L.A. Connection* took the dubbed version of *Cyrano de Bergerac* out of the dungeon and back into the theater with Skov introducing the film. That's the version that sold, but not the version that made it to the air.

Mad Movies with the L.A. Connection ran for one season with twenty-five episodes airing from September 1985 to December 1986, with re-runs the following year in syndication.

From the Four Star library, the troupe chose films to re-dub that spanned over thirty years. The films ranged from comedy to horror to detective films; some hailed as classics (*Nothing Sacred*) while others haven't fared so well (*Zorro's Fighting Legion*). "Folks at Four Star said, 'Here you go, here's access to the film vault,' keeping in mind that Four Star wanted the L.A. Connection to use films that were in the public domain or didn't have any kind of encumbrances as far as rights went," says Producer Randy Ridges. "There are some dogs in there, frankly, that I think they had to take because they could only get the films for free."

Episodes of *Mad Movies with the L.A. Connection* ran roughly twenty-two minutes long without commercials. Each had wraparound bits running about three minutes with nineteen episodes boasting an additional bit called "Home Movies" where, as the title implies, a clip from a home movie would be dubbed. These clips initially came from cast and crew members until the show began to air and viewers would submit their own to the show. That could leave as little as seventeen or eighteen minutes where the L.A. Connection would re-edit, re-dub, and re-contextualize a feature-length film for the show.

Skov continues, "With *Mad Movies with the L.A. Connection,* we had to write storylines to keep people interested for the episode. If you're writing for a clip, like we did with the Alan Thicke show, you don't have to. Sure, we'd create little stories for those, too, but you didn't have to be as story-intensive because the audience would only watch for less than five minutes. All you had to worry about was making it funny. It was a different kind of writing for *Mad Movies with the L.A. Connection.* Luckily, we had started by dubbing full-length movies. We were learning about creating a story for a longer period of time. That made it a lot easier when we only had to write roughly seventeen minutes of story. The hardest part was editing it and figuring out the direction you wanted to story to go before you started editing the film. Getting a full-length movie down to seventeen minutes takes a lot of thought, a lot of concentration, and a lot of planning before you even get to the writing phase.

"Those were some of the things I feel like I learned by mixing the movies. I learned how to edit and cut. When we started with *Mad Movies with the L.A. Connection,* of course, it was all analog. You couldn't do some of the stuff you can do now. You couldn't digitally remove anything like a sound hit or a voice-over. You couldn't even tighten up a voice-over. If we were out of synch, we were out of synch. Sometimes you could slightly adjust a line but it wasn't easy; it was tedious. What we did was time-consuming and not at all cost-effective. Nowadays, you can fix almost everything in post-production. If someone is out of synch you can move their line digitally and even cut off a little sound if you need to make it fit. It's amazing."

As the show's Producer, Associate Director, Stage Manager, and Post-Production Supervisor, Randy Ridges played a key role in getting the raw materials for each episode. "Back in those days, it was pretty primitive. I spent a lot of time ordering up film prints to be delivered to a post-production facility and transferred to video tape. I would supervise the film-to-tape transfers. I would get a time-coded ¾" videocassette. We would call them 'sub-masters.' I would prepare that and give it to the writers."

Trade ad for Mad Movies

Skov says, "Depending on how much time we all had, we would try to sit down together to watch the movie and come up with ideas. I would take those and come up with a final idea and put together an initial edit. We'd sit down and look at the film again with the storyline idea in mind. Then we would make edits based on 'what if we put this here and that there' to tighten up the story. Then, either I would give Randy Ridges our time code numbers or sometimes I'd do the edit myself.

"Once we had the final edit we would write our copy. We might make adjustments based on the edit or we might say, 'You know what? That isn't as funny as we thought. Let's get a little more footage and put it in here and change that up a little bit.' We could do whatever we wanted with the ¾" tapes. The final step was going into the post house and doing the final edit of the video, record the voice-over, and add that to the master.

"For the audio, you would have three tracks on a 1" master: one for your dialogue, one for your music, sound effects, laughter and all that. The third was audible time code. When you're in the studio, everything is separate, but then you'd have to designate them as one track or the other when you put them on the master. We would keep the dialogue apart from the rest so we could make adjustments like making it louder. You know, if you went from one city to another – and who knows what their systems would be – you could ride the audio. Hopefully, they never have to do that but, if you had to, you could.

"A lot of people think that just because you're taking something that's already there that there's no cost. They don't realize that it's actually almost more costly to do what we do than to go out and re-shoot it. Because, with shooting it, I've already got the audio, I've got the sound effects, I've got the visuals the way we want them. It's more time-consuming to do what we do. They don't factor in the cost of writing it, editing it, going to a recording studio, mixing it, put in all the Foley, bringing in music; everything you have to do for every television show, but we have to replace all the dialogue, as well.

"With the Foley, you can't just use sound effects because they'll never match. I used to use two Styrofoam cups for a horse's hooves. I mean, if a guy pulls his keys out of his pocket or a woman snaps her purse, if they got up out of a chair we'd put a little squeak in the chair. The things that most people try to remove, we would put back in because we had to create a soundtrack that sounded real. These days you see a lot of movies and say there's a guy on a train. You don't even hear the train; you just hear the guy's thoughts. Everything is so low behind it. We would put all that stuff in and make it rich to add to that verisimilitude. Some people would tune in and not even realize that the soundtrack had been replaced for a while. Over the years I've heard from a lot of people who have stumbled onto the show and by the time they realized what was going on, we had them.

"For me, it's always easier to write something if someone gives me footage. If somebody says, 'Here's *The Little Princess*, go do something with that.' That's easier than saying, 'Just go write a movie,' because I'm already halfway there. I've got the material, now I just have to make something out of it. The material dictates what I write which makes it easier for me to be funny. The harder part is, at least in terms of what we did, is to write the stuff where you're creating a story.

"We would all write together and not everybody wrote every episode. I was in charge of every episode and I would often give suggestions about tightening up or reworking bits that I didn't think were working. Stuff would always have to go by me. I had the final say. My job as the head writer and director was to listen to everybody's opinions and try to take what was the funniest. We had seven writers on the show and everybody was giving me their input. Sometimes I'd have to say, 'No, we're going in this direction.'"

A total of ten writers were credited for *Reefer Madness II*. Many of these people would go on to work on *Mad Movies with the L.A. Connection*, listed as "researchers" in the final credits. These include Ken Segall, writer of *Pink Panther & Pals*, John P. McCann, writer/actor in *Animaniacs*, and Bob Petrella producer of *Ice Road Truckers*. Other researchers included Ted Hardwick (*The Insider's Guide to Film School*) and April Winchell (*Who Framed Roger Rabbit?*).

Winchell recounts that "the researchers actually helped write that show, but Kent said he didn't have money in the budget for so many writers." As members of the L.A. Connection, the researchers also had to pay dues to be part of the group. "We were young, naïve, and so happy to work on a TV show that we didn't question the arrangement.

"In order to be on *Mad Movies with the L.A. Connection*, I had to join American Federation of Television and Radio Artists (AFTRA). I assumed I could do the same with the Writers Guild of America (WGA), and that's why I called them. When I realized the can of worms I opened, it was too late. The WGA called me in and asked me to explain my duties on the show, and that led to an investigation on behalf of all the researchers."[26]

"We had four main writers, who were all assigned to different shows: me, Connie, Bob, and Steve," recalls Skov. "Steve Pinto worked well with Connie, Bob and Steve Rollman worked well together. And, then, Connie. Steve Rollman and I wrote some

The researchers are revolting.

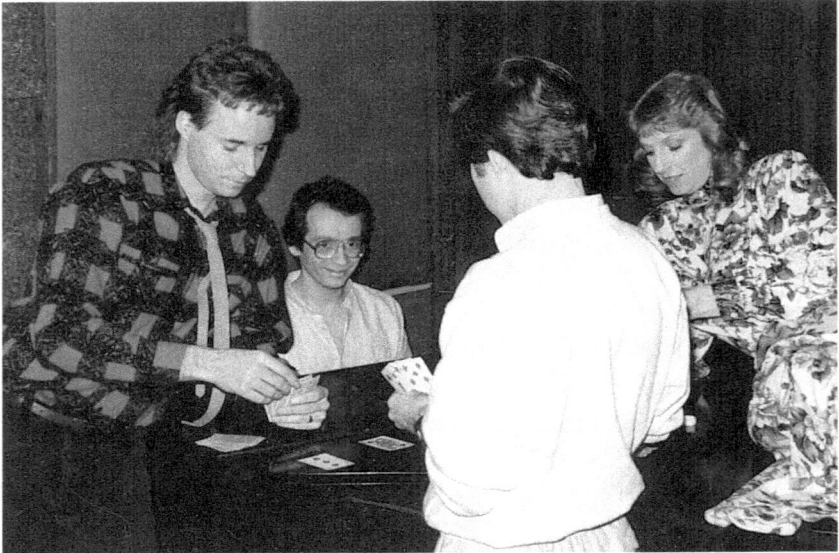

The cast playing cards.

together. But, even if you weren't a writer of the project, as a performer they can legally come in and change lines so you get the
input from everybody. It was really a budgetary situation. Four Star
couldn't afford to pay five writers for every show so they worked it
out where on the first thirteen shows I wrote as an individual, and

the others wrote as a team. The second thirteen shows were written as a team, with Bob and Steve Rollman. But, again, everybody had some input on every script because we all wanted to be part of it as a team and were all regular actors so, naturally, everybody contributed in different ways even if they weren't instrumental in writing from the script from the beginning to the end."

Steve Pinto says, "I think the first half of movies were the best because we didn't know if there would be a second half. So we started with the best choices. I still think *The Little Princess* is one of the better movies. *Cyrano de Bergerac* was very good and so was *Inspector General*. *Sherlock Holmes and the Secret Weapon* was just plain silly, turning this serious iconic character of classic literature into a bit of a dunce. The 'this is paper?' scene is brilliant. Of course, I wrote it. The best part of the job was writing jokes with your best friends. Who wouldn't like that? Sitting around making each other laugh."

"It's an awful fun business to be involved with," says Bob Buchholz, "But it's still a job. You still have to get up and go to work at nine o'clock in the morning. It was a difficult process, but we always had a good time. One thing about being involved in comedy is that you pretty much laugh throughout the day. Not everything is hysterical but you come up with ideas and bounce them off one another."

Skov says, "We were all really close; it was a very good group of people. That doesn't mean that we didn't argue. You could sit in our writing sessions and sometimes we'd just tell each other, 'You're an idiot. That's the stupidest thing I've ever heard.' You had to have a thick skin. I remember one time we had Will Ferrell come in. He did *Plan 9 from Outer Space*. I think it was me, Pinto, and a couple of other people, and we still talked like that. Will was just looking at us like, 'Who are these people?' We'd say a line and someone else would say, 'That's not funny, that's stupid! He wouldn't say that!' But we all really appreciated each other."

Skov continued, "We wrote things many different ways. Sometimes we just improvised to see where it would go based on a plot idea. The whole cast had slightly different senses of humor. Some of them were more pun-driven, some were more story-driven, some more character-driven. Some were just kind of wacky and weird while others were trying to be more intelligent. I'm kind of in the middle between all of them. Of everyone, I think I was probably

Man on the street interviews.

the most raucous and irreverent. I tried to put some edgy stuff into *Mad Movies with the L.A. Connection*. Obviously, we couldn't go as far as we could when we'd do a live movie. That's where you would see the rowdiness a lot more, because you could swear and make more sexual jokes. The crowd liked that. Not that the whole thing was driven that way but we went a lot further because it took a lot more to get censored.

"The thing about sex jokes in our style; most of it was innuendo. We'd get it as adults but most kids would have no idea even though they'd still laugh and think it's funny. We would make a reference to a dick as some other name for it. Or the women started calling breasts 'ta-tas.' You know, something you could get away with while knowing that people would laugh at it.

"One of the things we also tried to do is make the show fast, really fast-paced. I look at it now and go, 'Man, we went through those scenes fast.' I don't think we had any scenes longer than two minutes. Most of them were a minute, tops. Maybe there were a few in the first episode, but not too many. We wanted to make it fast-paced, too, because that's how everything was packed back then. The generations were changing. With the introduction of MTV, people's attention spans started shifting."

Skov also strove to keep *Mad Movies with the L.A. Connection* fairly timeless. Unlike the live shows where the L.A. Connection would constantly rewrite their plot lines for the times, keeping the material timely and trendy,[27] Skov says, "We tried to write them so that the jokes would last forever. If we do a takeoff on *The Exorcist* in *The Little Princess*, we know it's a movie so famous that people would always remember it. And there will always be other movies that deal with exorcism at some point in our life. We did *The Wizard of Oz* as a takeoff in *Nothing Sacred* because it's another classic movie. The takeoff on dating, you know, because there's always going to be dating. You try to pick subjects like Cyrano trying to get a job. That's a perfect subject for today! Some of the subject matter, like people trying to crash a party in *Night of the Living Dead,* is just universal. We tried to take classic stories or classic ideas or stuff that was popular that we thought would still be popular in fifteen or twenty years. Like we did a takeoff of Danny Kaye where everyone thought he was Michael Jackson in *The Inspector General*. We saw how big Michael Jackson was and figured he'd still be big later on.

"It makes me feel good to look back and see how well things are holding up. There's an occasional joke that's dated – a reference to a television show or time period thing – but not many. We tried not to have too many in there just because of that reason and we always

Promotional photo.

wrote with that in mind. Let's be funny forever instead of being funny now and not funny later."

Says Pinto, "You know you have a success when it is still funny today. To this day we still quote lines from the show whenever it fits the context of what's happening at the moment. That's the sign of good writing."

One of the funniest things about *Mad Movies with the L.A. Connection* was the voices the L.A. Connection provided the on-screen characters. Skov says, "You look at the characters and think of what voice you're going to do. What voice would fit that character? When we did *The Stranger*, I didn't do an Orson Welles impression but I did do an Orson Welles-type voice. And then you have to be able to make the voice you choose match the mouth movements. Edward G. Robinson gave more expression with his mouth than other characters that tend to mumble more. That's where it gets harder.

"You have to be specific in your writing so that the words match the lip movements and create a story and make it funny. That's why a lot of people aren't doing what we did, because all of that prohibits them from making it good. People can do a voice-over and make it funny because there's no lip synch, but when you get down to lip synch it becomes a whole different element of trying to tell a story

Promotional photo with an easily-swapped episode image.

and make the lip synch perfect and have a character voice that people want to listen to for the duration."

Steve Pinto says, "The hardest part about this dubbing process is coming up with a plot, fitting dialogue to lip smacks while making that dialogue progress the narrative *and* be funny. We always looked for scenes that had action or body movements to play off instead of just talking heads."

Skov remembers, "I enjoyed playing the lead in *Outpost in Morocco*; George Raft, and I really enjoyed doing Roy Rogers in *Under California Stars*. I thought he was a clever character to do and a lot of fun. I had to send that episode out to Roy Rogers before it aired and he thought it was hysterical. Those are the kinds of compliments I like. I made him kind of a silly guy, you know, a loving silly guy. So the real Roy Rogers couldn't have been too upset about that. I had a voice I liked to do that I called 'Real Dumb Guy,' he was always a lot of fun. I had kind of done him in two movies, *Attack of the 50 Foot Woman*, which was the first movie I did. I got to play the deputy and did that voice. I also did him in *Cat-Women of the Moon*, too. I did the second co-pilot in that voice and it really worked for me. People loved the voice. He was always so stupid that I was able to get away with saying all sorts of really stupid stuff."

Steve Pinto remembers being happy doing impressions of "Ronald Reagan, Edward G. Robinson, Vincent Price, James Mason, and Basil Rathbone, names I grew up with – not because I'm that old. They were still prominent in Hollywood and their movies are classics. My impressionist role models, Rich Little, John Byner, and Frank Gorshin, did them in their acts. Nowadays, if you mention these names to anyone born after 1985, they just look at you."

Randy Ridges said, "Once we had everything in the can—Kent's wraparounds, as well as the cut down of the film—I did all of the post production. I took everything into the video tape facility, did all the post, the title cards. Pretty much I remember eighteen to twenty-hour days for four, five, six days in a row. I think we cranked out an episode every ten days to two weeks.

"As far as the wraparounds, which was when Kent was out on location, doing his intro and the set-up for the film," says Randy Ridges, "I worked on getting permits, on getting whatever props were needed, hired the technical people – camera, sound, lights, that sort of thing. Some of the stuff we did we had no budget for. It was a lot of location shooting and what we called 'guerrilla television' because we just didn't have money to do it like a Union shoot would do.

"Every episode we did was probably hundreds of hours of production and, mostly, post-production," says Ridges. "We might have scheduled Kent to do wraparound shoots back to back, but we never used the same location twice. Kent was his own director so we pretty much stood back and let him do his own thing."

Skov says, "Shooting wraparounds, I mean, I didn't care about that. It was okay for me. I did it because they made me. That wasn't the most fun thing to do but, you know, I enjoyed doing them. I also enjoyed doing the actual mixing and recording, putting in the laughs and the music.

"For our live shows, we almost always used Matt Davis for keyboards. He was a real pleasure to work with. He was a very talented guy with kind of a corny, campy system that fit perfectly with the kind of stuff we did. With *Mad Movies with the L.A. Connection*, we used Richard Baker. He was Carlos Santana's keyboard player [from 1980-1982]. His wife, Mary Newland, sang our theme song. When Mary was younger, she was out of Canada and would come to Detroit

Kent with Mary Newland (and friend).

to be a groupie for all these bands, and I think one of them was Carlos Santana, and that's how they met.

"I don't remember how I found him, but Richard didn't want to go on tour anymore after a while. His style was a little slicker. Every episode of *Mad Movies with the L.A. Connection* has a different sound to it. Matt was probably hurt a little bit that I didn't give him the *Mad Movies with the L.A. Connection* gig, but he didn't have the stability and stamina that Richard had. That was a tough decision, but when Carlos Santana's keyboard player became available, that made it a little easier. It worked out great with Richard, and Matt continued to do the live shows with us.

If *Mad Movies with the L.A. Connection* suffers from anything, it's the use of a laugh track. This audio flourish is something of a holdover from the days of the L.A. Connection's live performances. Skov says, "There's a thrill you get from the response an audience gives you when you do it live. The one criticism I got from a critic of *Mad Movies with the L.A. Connection* was that it didn't translate the same on television as when we were sitting with a live audience. I got that same thing from executives, who were trying to give us a reason why they maybe didn't want to pick us up. I'll grant that, perhaps, if we did *Mad Movies with the L.A. Connection* again that it might be smart to do it in front of a live audience because that gives it a little more feeling. It's like watching a concert with an audience rather than just listening to a studio performance. You feed off the energy of the crowds.

"There's something that you're leaving behind versus a live event that just comes and goes. The live events served as fantastic jumping grounds for us to launch the whole L.A. Connection and do all the stuff we've done. There's nothing more thrilling than doing a live performance. With 700 or 800 people out there watching you, it's wonderful. Nothing can compare. When you're in the studio and doing all the work of editing and writing, it's fun but without the performance of it.

"I enjoy making the episodes, but the performance was the ultimate. You can't replace that endorphin rush, that energy. I'm sure any performer would tell you the same thing. You can't replace being on stage or in front of a crowd, especially if you are in the comedy business where you get to hear laughter. You wrote those lines and you're not sure if they're going to be funny or not, and then the response you get is so positive. You go back as writers and you go, 'Wow.' You didn't think that was going to be funny. Or, 'That was one that I wrote?' Or, 'Geez, God, that one fell flat. We all thought that was going to work, and that just kind of didn't work. Weird. Why didn't that work?' And then other ones just work unbelievably, ones we thought were going to work, and that's just so rewarding, you know, that you are able to see.

"Doing the live show helped us write *Mad Movies with the L.A. Connection* because we all got our sense of humor about the movie dubbing based on the response we got from when we had all written together. Even with 'Flicke of the Night,' I was able to get a more immediate response because they were being performed in front of a live audience, even though they were done to tape. Occasionally, I'd do the same thing and take clips we'd written for our sizzle reels and put them up on screen, usually on New Year's Eve, just to see how the audience would respond. I'd think, 'Okay, good, that works.' And, you always know when you go into an executives' office and play a tape what they'll laugh at. It's fairly consistent.

"We did some of the same films we did on the show, like *Shock*, in front of a live audience. When I added laughs to the show, I could do this where we had gotten our laughs live. But for the movies we never did live; I had to add the laughs in where I thought they would be, based on our experiences. 'They laughed at this in the live show; let's see if this will work here.'

"Not having that immediate feedback to the show was a bit daunting. We thought we were doing a good thing, but, when we were cancelled we said, 'Okay, maybe it was just not as funny as we thought it was going to be.' Some people would say that maybe there's just something about a live event, that when you're there it's more exciting and they know that you're in the front row and making stuff up, improvising, even if it's scripted. Those live events are a one-time thing. There's a different relationship with the audience. It's just for them. There's a different kind of laughter that comes out of a live event versus a *Mad Movies with the L.A. Connection* show where we manufactured the laughter and put it on television in hopes of people liking it."

Episode Guide

Mad Movies with the L.A. Connection ran for twenty-six episodes. The show ran from the fall of 1985 to the summer of 1986. When available, dates for the shows listed were taken from the *Boca Raton News*.

Cast looking right... mostly.

Episode #100: "Cyrano de Bergerac" (1950)
Air Date: 10/12/85

Jose Ferrer plays the famous poet who becomes a job-hungry ego-maniac in this version.

Host Segment: Kent tries to keep up with current fashions by wearing a cape.

Vox Poll: Have you seen Cyrano de Bergerac and what you remember about it?

Behind the scenes on Cyrano.

Best Answer: "I thought this was the line for Indiana Jones and the Temple of Doom."
Promo: Clip from the Four Star TV show "Wanted: Dead or Alive."
Home Movie: An alien invasion.
Note: Episode includes a final preview segment for Sherlock Holmes and the Secret Weapon.
Writers: Ken Segall & Kent Skov
John McCann recalls "This is the only episode that I worked on. Around this time I had a death in the family and had to go back out East and liquidate an estate."

Episode #101: Santa Fe Trail (1940)

Air Date: 10/6/85
Ron Reagan Jr. has a nightmare that his father (Ronald Reagan) is running against Abraham Lincoln for the Presidency.
Host Segment: Theatrical hijinks including a Reagan standee making an appearance at the Nuart.
Vox Poll: "Who would you vote for if Abe Lincoln were running for president against Ronald Reagan?"
Best Answer: "Ron Reagan, he's alive."
Promo: Scene from *Under California Stars*.
Home Movie: A young scientist's life story.
Writers: Connie Sue Cook, Steve Pinto & Kent Skov

Episode #102: The Little Princess (1939)

Original Air Date: 2/2/86
Shirley Temple is possessed by a doll, and only a song-and-dance exorcism can save her.
Host Segment: Kent takes in a Shirley Temple with a Shirley Temple.
Vox Poll: "What was Shirley Temple the little princess of?"
Best Answer: "I don't go back as far as Shirley Temple."
Promo: Scene from *Shock*.
Home Movie: An immigrant's tale.
Writers: Connie Sue Cook, Steve Pinto & Kent Skov

Note: Includes a preview for *Nothing Sacred*. Additional voices by April Winchell. The Shirley Temple lookalike was Lauren Gulbrand.

Steve Pinto recalls, "We were writing *The Little Princess* where, in our version, Shirley Temple is possessed and her little doll is the devil (I played the doll). Well, there was a joke about wolfs bane and Kent didn't know what that is, so it wasn't going in. We had to take a poll of all the office staff. 'Have you ever heard of wolfs bane?' Kent eventually relented and it made the final cut. Whew.

"For some reason Kent and I had different senses of humor and he would veto some of my brilliant ideas. So I would have Bob [Buchholz] play 'the front' and present the ideas as his own to Kent who would readily accept them. Go figure."

Kent recalls, "This was our first episode and we actually had some audio issues in the wraparounds that we corrected from that point on. From people's response, I think this is our most popular episode."

Episode #103: A Star Is Born (1937)
Original Air Date: 9/29/85
Janet Gaynor searches for Mr. Right.
Host Segment: Kent visits a video dating service.
Vox Poll: "Who is your ideal mate?"
Best Answer: "One that goes out of town a lot."
Promo: Scene from *Sherlock Holmes and the Secret Weapon*.
Home Movie: The story of a despot.
Writers: Connie Sue Cook, Steve Pinto & Kent Skov
Note: Includes a preview of *Santa Fe Trail*.

Episode #104: Shock (1946)
Original Air Date: 11/10/85
The only two-episode parodies the lust, intrigue, and murder of a soap opera, and finds a doctor (Vincent Price) who still makes house calls!
Host Segment: Kent works as an EMS worker.
Vox Poll: "What shocks you?"
Best Answer: "Electricity."

Promo: Scene from *The Inspector General.*
Home Movie: A survey of nature's oddities.
Writers: Connie Sue Cook, Steve Pinto & Kent Skov
Note: Features an "interview" with Vincent Price wherein Kent asks questions that Price "answers" via clips.
Randy Ridges recalls, "We shot at my mother's house. We rented an ambulance and had it pull into my mother's house, into her

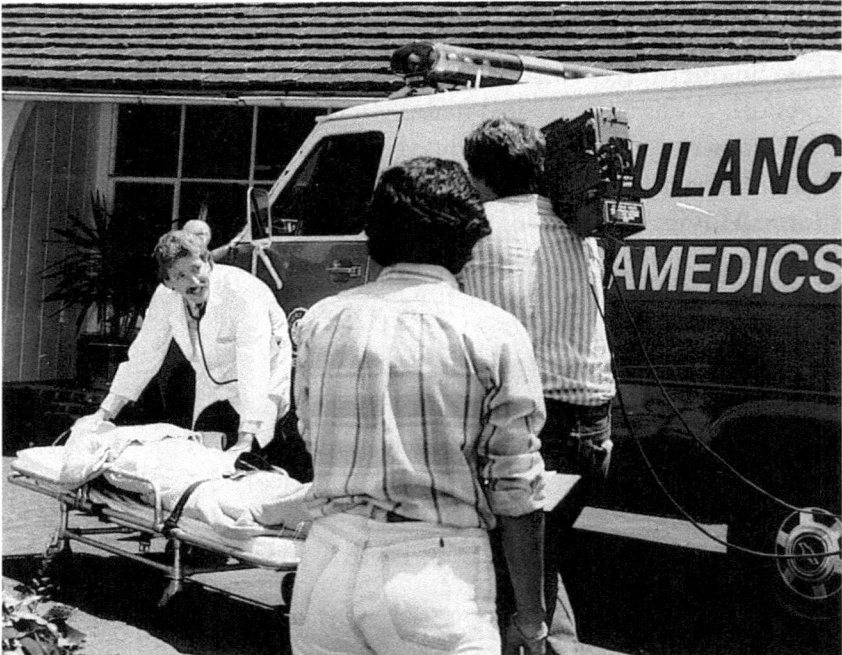

driveway. The neighbors got really upset because they thought it was a real ambulance and were wondering what had happened at the house."

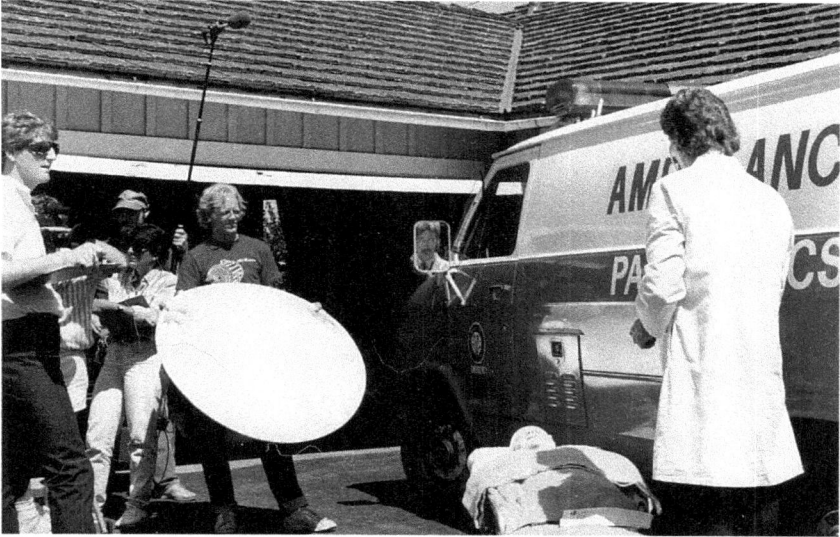

Behind the scenes on Shock.

Episode #105: Shock (1946)
Original Air Date: 11/17/85
Part two of *Shock*.
Host Segment: Kent interviews Annabelle Shaw.

Promo: Scene from *Doll Face*.
Home Movie: A documentary about the Dog Man of Alcatraz.
Writers: Connie Sue Cook, Steve Pinto & Kent Skov
Note: Features a preview of *The Inspector General*.
Kent recalls, "Annabelle Shaw had a very good laugh, and she was quite fun. She was so far removed at this point from show biz. She was just kind of a regular Joe."

Working with Annabelle Shaw on Shock.

Episode #106: Night of the Living Dead (1968)

Original Air Date: 12/8/85

A party with no food or drink becomes a wild free-for-all for Judith O'Dea and Duane Jones.

Host Segment: Kent prepares for a dinner party with Harry Medved (brother of Michael), co-creator of the Golden Turkey Awards.

Promo: Scene from *The Little Princess*

Home Movie: Years before Hogwarts, we see a film about a school for young magicians.

Writers: Connie Sue Cook, Steve Pinto & Kent Skov

Kent recalls, "Harry Medved was very informative about movies. I had run into the Medved brothers before because they had written about us, because we started dubbing movies and their career was ascending as ours was at that time. You know, Harry Medved was a critic, but mainly of B-movies, weird stuff, and off-type turkey books and things like that. And that's why we brought him on, because we knew he'd be a good interview. We thought that kind of a B-movie that got cult status. And, of course, he went on to pretty mainstream media where he talked about a lot of stuff after that."

Episode #107: Nothing Sacred (1937)

Original Air Date: 9/27/85

A woman (Carole Lombard) hires a detective (Fredric March) to locate her friends over the rainbow.

Host Segment: Kent tries to get to Kansas via a hot air balloon.

Vox Poll: "What's your favorite *Wizard of Oz* character and why?"

Best Answer: "The coroner of Munchkin land."

Promo: Scene from *The Inspector General*.

Home Movie: A super spy eludes capture.

Writers: Connie Sue Cook, Steve Pinto & Kent Skov

Randy Ridges recalls, "We had Kent in a hot air balloon at some community college. We didn't have authorization to let it fly without a tether so we had to shoot it at an angle to make it look like Kent was flying away, though he really wasn't."

Episode #108: Sherlock Holmes and the Secret Weapon (1943)
Original Air Date: 10/26/85

Holmes and Watson (Basil Rathbone, Nigel Bruce) are hired to stop a conspiracy from stealing library books and selling them on the black market.

Host Segment: Kent finds intrigue in the library.
Vox Poll: "What's the punishment for people who keep their library books too long?"
Best Answer: "Set off a bomb that goes off on the day they're due."
Promo: Scene from *Nothing Sacred*.
Home Movie: An alien baby infiltrates Earth.
Writers: Connie Sue Cook, Steve Pinto & Kent Skov

Episode #109: Doll Face (1946)
Original Air Date: 11/2/85

A behind-the-scenes look at the world of beauty contests, with Vivian Blaine, Dennis O'Keefe, Perry Como and Carmen Miranda.

Host Segment: Kent interacts with the sole finalist in the Doll Face contest (Connie Sue Cook).
Vox Poll: What kind of "Miss Competition" would you like to see?
Best Answer: "I'd like to see a hit and miss pageant."
Promo: Scene from *Cyrano de Bergerac*.
Home Movie: A commercial for Beer Beach.

Writers: Connie Sue Cook, Steve Pinto & Kent Skov
Note: Includes preview for *Under California Stars*. Additional voices by Rachel Lujean.

Connie as Carmen Miranda.

Episode #110: Under California Stars (1948)

A compulsive gambler (Roy Rogers) cannot control his urges.
Host Segment: Kent visits "Rancho Mad Movie" to hang out with Trigger's relative.
Promo: Scene from *Doll Face*.
Home Movie: The giant who helped shape America.
Writers: Connie Sue Cook, Steve Pinto & Kent Skov
Note: Includes preview for *Shock*. Paul Rugg narrated the home movie for this episode.
Kent recalls, "We didn't have any bad guests except for that horse. There were flies everywhere!"

Episode #111: My Favorite Brunette (1947)

In a spoof of this Bob Hope classic, the head of a gangster family receives a death threat.
Host Segment: Kent's at the Mad Movies Body Shop to pick up the comedy limo.
Promo: Scene from *My Favorite Brunette*.
Home Movie: The shady Buck Brothers go on a rampage of crime and savagery.
Writers: Connie Sue Cook, Steve Pinto & Kent Skov
Note: Additional voices by David Leon

Episode #112: Outpost in Morocco (1949)

Original Air Date: 12/1/85
A spy thriller in which the hero pulls the plug on water thieves.
Host Segment: Kent co-hosts with Marie Windsor
Promo: Scene from *Doll Face*.
Home Movie: The tale of "Little Olga," a famous Russian gymnast.
Writers: Connie Sue Cook, Steve Pinto & Kent Skov
Note: Additional voices by Bob Petrella
Kent recalls, "Marie Windsor was a lot of fun. She had a good sense of humor about her, and she was still very sexy for a woman of sixty-five at the time. She still had that Hollywood glamour kind of sex appeal to her. She still was working in the business; not a lot, but she was working."

Episode #113: The Inspector General (1949)
Original Air Date: 11/24/85
Danny Kaye rocks a military look as a pop star from the past.
Host Segment: Kent hangs out at a record store.
Vox Poll: What star do you look like?
Best Answer: "They tell me I look like Princess Di in the morning but by late afternoon or evening, I look like Robert Redford."
Promo: Scene from *Sherlock Holmes and the Secret Weapon*.
Home Movie: Uncle Lee invents huge food.
Writers: Connie Sue Cook, Steve Pinto & Kent Skov
Note: Additional voices by Ted Hardwick

Behind the scenes of The Inspector General.

Episode #114: D.O.A. (1950)
In a spoof of *I Love Lucy*, Rico Ricardo (Edmund O'Brien) searches for his missing wife and winds up falling in love with his wife's friend Ethel.
Host Segment: Kent's at the Tropicana Hotel, Tropicana liquor store, Duke's Tropicana coffee shop, and the Hollywood Tropicana night club.

Home Movie: Rags to Riches: A family wins a talent contest and is jettisoned to fame and fortune.
Writers: Bob Buchholz and Stephen L. Rollman
Note: Additional voices by April Winchell. Beginning with this episode, the Vox Poll has been retired and all promos for the show are scenes from the movie being dubbed that week.

Behind the scenes of DOA.

Episode #115: The Stranger (1946)
A sleazy tabloid editor (Edward G. Robinson) wants to make former hunchback Quasimodo (Orson Welles) the subject of an article.
Host Segment: Kent checks out the latest episode of *Peep-Hole* magazine at a newsstand.
Home Movie: Christmas Land: In the village of Kringle, Christmas is celebrated every day.
Writers: Connie Sue Cook, Steve Pinto & Kent Skov
Note: Additional voices by Doug Requa.

Episode #116: This is the Army (1943)
In this Irving Berlin musical, President Reagan decides to reenlist in order to supervise things from the inside.

Host Segment: Kent visits an Army prop storage facility.
Home Movie: Future Wives: A documentary about the challenges faced by women in the Space Age.
Writers: Bob Buchholz and Stephen L. Rollman

Behind the scenes of This is the Army.

Episode #117: Beneath the 12-Mile Reef (1953)

Jack Cousteau (Gilbert Roland) and crew try to stop marauders from stripping the ocean floor of the endangered sea brain.

Host Segment: Kent goes yachting with Terry Moore, one of the original stars of *Beneath the 12-Mile Reef*.

Home Movie: The Rainmaker: Three scientists can't induce the rain but a mystical gardener brings water to the land.

Writers: Bob Buchholz and Stephen L. Rollman

Note: Additional voices by Todd Torick

Kent recalls, "Terry Moore was quite nice. I got to hear some great stories from her about Howard Hughes. That was the same episode where I got sick down below, so, we didn't get to talk quite as much as I would have liked to because I was just trying to recover."

Behind the scenes of Beneath the 12-Mile Reef.

Episode #118: The Perils of Pauline (1947)

Against her husband's (John Lund) wishes, Pauline (Betty Hutton) runs for mayor.

Host Segment: Kent's at the Pauline campaign office.

Home Movie: Home Entertainment: A commercial for the do-it-yourself entertainment kit.

Writers: Bob Buchholz and Stephen L. Rollman

Note: Additional voices by April Winchell

Episode #119: Decameron Nights (1953)

The not so "happily-ever-after" part of romance is seen when Cinderella (Joan Fontaine) and her prince (Louis Jourdan) experience marital problems.

Host Segment: Kent's cleans out the attic, turns into a frog.

Home Movie: Baby-Robics: The latest aerobics craze has people working out like toddlers.

Writers: Kent Skov

Note: Additional voices by April Winchell

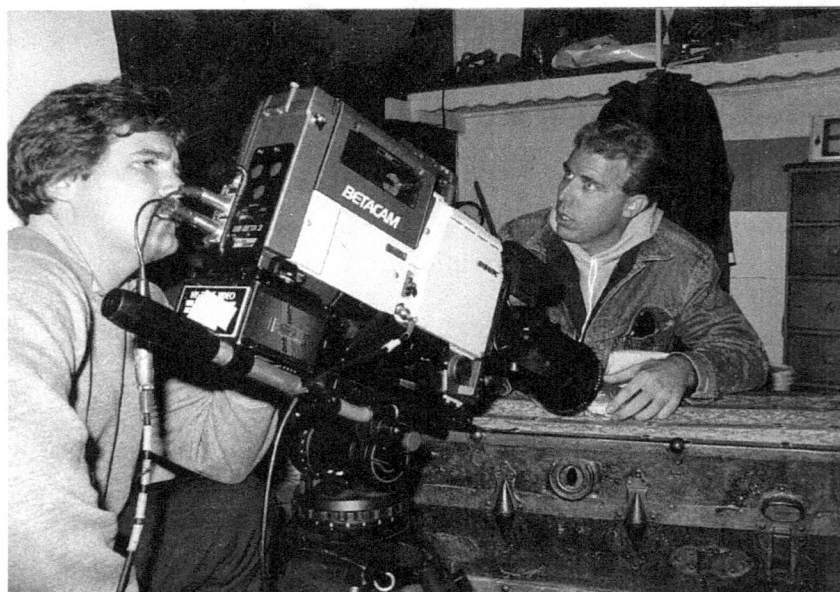

Behind the scenes of Decameron Nights.

Episode #120: Captain Scarlett (1953)

No one is safe when Robin Hood, Red Riding Hood, and Captain Scarlett (Richard Greene, Leonora Amar, Nedrick Young) join forces to fight tyranny.

Host Segment: Kent enjoys the great outdoors.
Home Movie: Oddities II: Another mondo documentary about the stranger corners of the world.
Writers: Bob Buchholz and Stephen L. Rollman
Note: Additional voices by Ted Hardwick

Episode #121: The Outlaw (1943)

Billy the Kid, Bat Masterson and Doc Holliday (Jack Buetel, Thomas Mitchell, and Walter Huston) rub elbows in this version of Howard Hughes's film.
Host Segment: Kent's back at the ranch, preparing for a show down with The Kid (Craig Cignarelli).
Home Movie: Un-Electric Cowboy: A disgrace to his spurs, the Un-Electric blows his chance at a rodeo.
Writers: Bob Buchholz and Stephen L. Rollman
Note: Additional voices by Roz Turem. The Kid character was played the son of Four Star International's head of distribution. Craig Cignarelli would find himself in the spotlight in the early 1990s in regard to the infamous Menendez murder trial. Craig testified to a grand jury that Erik Menendez confessed to parricide.[28] Ironically, on July 22, 1983, the head of Four Star International, Henry Harrison Kyle, had been slain by his own son.[29]

Behind the scenes of The Outlaw.

Episode #122: Zorro's Fighting Legion (1939)

The masked avenger (Reed Hadley) faces a deadly challenge from a mechanical villain.

Host Segment: Kent continuously misses interview opportunities with Zorro.

Home Movie: Zombie Kids: A plague of undead youths spring forth from the ocean.

Writers: Bob Buchholz and Stephen L. Rollman

Note: Additional voices by Mitch Watson. This episode includes several shots from previously dubbed films (*Shock*, *My Favorite Brunette*, *The Little Princess*, etc.).

Episode #123: The Divorce of Lady X (1938)

Merle Oberon and Laurence Olivier have an affair.

Host Segment: Kent hangs out at hot spots for illicit assignations.

Home Movie: The Fable: Princess Athena becomes the first female astronaut.

Writers: Bob Buchholz and Stephen L. Rollman

Note: Additional voices by Nancy Van Anders

Episode #124: "Mad Movies Double Feature"

Dressed to Kill (1946)

Daniel Boone (1936)

The only double feature episode of *Mad Movies with the L.A. Connection* boasts two films about thievery. In *Dressed to Kill*, Sherlock Holmes and Dr. Watson pursue a gang of dwarf thieves while *Daniel Boone* (George O'Brien) looks for the hoods who stole his coonskin cap.

Host Segment: Kent's surrounded, briefly, by the accoutrements of Sherlock Holmes before heading out to the campfire. If only he'd looked in the window at the Holmes & Boone pawn shop.

Home Movie: Tiki Expedition: A perilous journey to a Tiki paradise.

Writers: Bob Buchholz and Stephen L. Rollman

Note: Additional voices by Ted Davis

Behind the scenes of the Mad Movies Double Feature.

Episode #125: "The Best of Mad Movies"
A clip show! The cast looks back at bits from previous films in the final episode.

Host Segment: Kent and the other members of the L.A. Connection are in the sound studio where episodes are recorded.

Home Movie: La Chica Ting-Ting: A Latina spitfire has critics raving.

Writers: Kent Skov

Note: Additional voices by April Winchell. The following on-screen message rolls at the end of the episode: "At this time, the L.A. Connection must apologize to its viewing public. While you have seen the real Kent Skov throughout the series, you have never heard the real Kent Skov. We have been dubbing his voice the entire time. THIS is how he really SOUNDS . . . ." This was followed by a re-dub of Kent with Connie Sue Cook's Shirley Temple voice over him.

Behind the scenes of The Best of Mad Movies

After Mad Movies

"We got a lot of good reviews for the show. I never saw a negative one. Howard Rosenberg called us one of TV's 'best kept secrets,'[30] but it's sad we were a secret. If more people knew about *Mad Movies with the L.A. Connection*, I think it would have been a success, even bigger, but there's only so many promotional dollars that Four Star had to spend. There's only so much that the local affiliates would do. Our show wasn't a *Cheers*. It wasn't a big show so they're not going to put that much into something that doesn't get big ratings," says Skov.

Along with Dick Cignarelli as the President of Distribution, Four Star International had Joe Fischer, formerly of Universal Studios, as the CEO. Both men worked to bring Four Star International back to profitability. According to *Broadcasting* magazine, the show was Four Star's "#1 attraction." Western sales director at Four Star International, David Reinbach, reported that sales of the show were "excellent," attributing the success of the show to its unique format. He said that the show had cleared twenty markets, including Post-Newsweek and the King Broadcasting groups, as well as WCCO-TV in Minneapolis.[31]

Skov recalls, "With some stations, it worked really well and they wanted to re-up and buy. Let's say that out of maybe 50 percent of the marketplace we were in, they could have resold it to probably 40 percent of them. That's pretty good. Four or five would renew and they could always go out and get new stuff."

While the first season of went on the air, the L.A. Connection continued to dub movies live, packing the theaters in which they played.

Producer and Jack-of-All-Trades Randy Ridges lent his skills to the live shows as well. "We travelled around; we went as far as San Diego and Santa Barbara. I ran the sound board for them. I had a blast and the audiences just ate that stuff up. They loved the live shows. It was pretty amazing to see. There was a lot of repeat business, especially at the Nuart Theater. It was like the phenomenon that happens with *The Rocky Horror Picture Show*. People would dress up like characters and they would repeat the lines.

SOLD IN 15 OF THE TOP 20 MARKETS!

(3)	CHICAGO	WTTW
(4)	PHILADELPHIA	WTAF
(6)	BOSTON	WNEV
(7)	DETROIT	WDIV
(9)	CLEVELAND	WOFO
(10)	DALLAS	KTXA
(11)	HOUSTON	KTXH
(13)	MIAMI	WPLG
(14)	MINNEAPOLIS	WCCO
(15)	SEATTLE	KING
(16)	ATLANTA	WSB
(17)	TAMPA	WTOG
(18)	ST. LOUIS	KONL
(19)	DENVER	KCNC
(20)	SACRAMENTO	KOVR

Mad Movies in the top markets.

"The big secret was, to anybody who had seen the live shows multiple times, that it was scripted even though it was supposedly adlibbed and it was a live dubbing. All of those guys, they knew what worked, and if they had a line that was good in one of those shows, you can bet they did it again. And, the audience would know it too, so on some of the best shows, people in the audience were screaming

Producer-Director-Creator
Kent Skov

**L.A.
CONNECTION**

13442 Ventura Blvd.
Sherman Oaks, Ca. 91423
(818) 784-1868

"New Comedy Cult Craze" L.A. Times

VARIOUS RATINGS
FROM MAD MOVIES WITH THE L.A. CONNECTION

DETROIT (NBC)	13/26	7:30 pm	9/14/85
	7.9/25	1:00 pm	9/21/85
	7.4/25	1:00 pm	10/19/85
	7/18	1:00 pm	1/4/86
	7/21	1:00 pm	Feb Sweeps 1986
BOSTON (CBS)	3.4/8	11:30 pm	9/14/85 (opposite Sat. Night Live)
	3.3/11	11:30 pm	9/28/85
	4.8/13	11:30 pm	10/5/85
	4.7/14	11:30 pm	10/12/85
	4.5/11	11:30 pm	10/19/85
	4/10	11:30 pm	1/4/86
CHICAGO (IND) CH 11	2.2/4	8:30 pm	10/12/85 (opposite Cheers)
	2/3	8:00 pm	10/17/85 (opposite Cosby)
	4/7	8:30 pm	1/4/86 (opposite Cheers)
PHILADELPHIA (IND) CH 29	2.9/6	9/28/85	9/28/85
	3.0/5	10/5/85	
	3.5/6	10/12/85	
	3.6/7	10/19/85	
	3.8/7	10/26/85	
MIAMI (ABC)	6/12	7:30 pm	9/14/85
	4.5/11	12:30 pm	9/21/85 (opposite Sat. Night Live)
	2.8/14	12:30 pm	10/26/85
HOUSTON (IND) CH 20	3.8/7	10:00 pm	10/5/85
	3.3/4	10:00 pm	10/12/85 (opposite Wrestling & Taxi)
	3.2/5	10:00 pm	10/19/85
	4/6	10:00 pm	1/4/86
DALLAS (IND) CH 21	3.2/-	10:00 pm	1/4/85

1 of 2

Mad Movies's Ratings.

out the lines as the same time as the actors. When the audience was on and the actors were on, it was just a great live show."

Steve Pinto adds, "We would play the same cartoon [Tex Avery's *Rock-A-Bye Bear*] before each show, no matter the movie. It was about a bear who was trying to get some sleep for the winter and things kept waking him up. Audiences came prepared for it. They knew the dialogue and would recite the good parts in unison. There was a point in the cartoon where a paper airplane was thrown.

Dozens—and I mean dozens—of paper airplanes would fly through the audience! It was like *The Rocky Horror Picture Show*. We knew we had a following.

"Live dubbing was like doing any live show. The nerves and butterflies would grow and grow just before show time. I didn't like the grand entrance of running down the aisles to the front row, but I guess it was theatrical. Once the film started, you're past that threshold and breathing again.

"When it came to live dubbing, I liked playing a handful of different incidental characters as opposed to playing just one main character. This way I got to do different voices and have more fun. *Cyrano* was always a favorite. It was funny and I played the Swedish baker among others. *Attack of the 50 Foot Woman* was an audience favorite. I played the sheriff, the doctor and the butler. Quite often I would have conversations with myself; i.e., two of my characters would talk with each other. Now that's hard. *Cat-Women of the Moon* I liked because there were only four men. I could relax and worry about only one character. It was a nice change.

Plan 9 from Outer Space was one we did many times over, for obvious reasons. It's been called the worst movie ever made. I played one of the 'spacemen,' with a German accent, who had what has since come to be known as 'the football speech.' The first time we did it live that speech went over so well I was always under a lot of pressure to repeat its success. Sometimes it's just not possible to capture lightning in a bottle a second time.

"I remember one time we were doing *Plan 9 from Outer Space* and two of my characters, the German spaceman and his leader who was a Truman Capote-type, were speaking with each other in the spaceship. Well, as happens with movie projectors, the film broke. The screen went dark right in the middle of my scene! I continued to play it as if there had been a power failure on the spaceship, you know, as when a fuse is blown and the lights go out: 'I'll get a flashlight. I'm gonna look out the window and see if it's the neighborhood or just us.' It went on for a few minutes 'till the movie started up again. The crowd loved it! They knew that was completely improvised."

Skov adds, "With our *Plan 9 from Outer Space* at the Nuart in West L.A., we got help again from KROQ. The DJ, Dusty Street, came in to do one of the voices, I think she did Vampira. She was terrible. But, KROQ helped us fill the audience up. That *Plan 9 from Outer Space* show also helped us get signed by the William Morrison Agency. It was one of those dream-type things. We saw this one guy in his seat, who was obviously not part of our audience. He was in a suit while the rest of us were in jeans. He came down just to look, to stare at me, and I'm going, 'What is this?' He hands me a card and says, 'Call me tomorrow. We want to sign you.'

"He came by my home office the next day and I showed him some clips. He said, 'My god, this is amazing, I want to sign you guys.' We signed and he introduced us to Joe Wizan, the former President of 20th Century Fox films. Wizan had just gone off and started his own company. One of the first deals he made was with the L.A. Connection to dub a movie. He started talking to Warner Bros. and they offered us $250,000.

"If we were going to do it Union, I was going to need $396,000. That was to hire all five writers through the Writers Guild, me as the director through the Directors Guild, and the musicians through the Musicians Union. We would have also had the Screen Actors Guild for the voices; they told me that if I wanted to add people in that I could add three voices. Then there's the production budget and other stuff you need. That was $396,000 minimum and they told me that they'll give me $250,000.

"I was on the phone with Barry Reardon and Joe Wizan and I said, 'I don't know if I can do it.' And Joe said, 'I'll give you the money right now.' I just don't know because then I can't hire my talent. 'What am I going to do?' I asked, 'Am I going to tell two or three of the guys that I can't hire them?' I don't want to get everybody mad at me that could affect future deals and cause some dissention. I'm very loyal to my people, which is why they stay with me for ten, thirteen, fifteen, thirty years. They know I'm not going to screw them over just to make a deal.

"Had I not turned down that Warner Bros. movie, I think that could have changed a lot of stuff, too, because then we would have gotten maybe an international reputation. If that movie just did moderately well, I think it would have led to more television shows. I think it would have changed a lot because people who watched what we did all liked it. We just had to let people know that it existed. When the show got to Nickelodeon, a million people a week were watching.

We started to get some heat again. The Ha! Channel and the Comedy Channel came along and they offered much less money. We weren't able to make a deal with them and, really, there weren't a lot of other places we could go at the time.

"We probably weren't going to be able to go back into syndication unless somebody wanted to syndicate us, and that route is harder because you are already there, and you have to come with a different kind of show. Cable was the next best thing but cable back then didn't have any money. They were only buying reruns; there wasn't that much original programming and, what there was, was really cheap.

"Rhino offered us a deal at one point. They said, 'We'll give you a couple thousand dollars.' We were all Union so there was no way we could do it for that. 'We'll give you the films so you don't have to pay for the films,' they said. I have to write it, go into the studio, pay the talent, and they wanted to give us a couple thousand bucks. 'But, we'll market it for you.' I couldn't do it.

"Years later, I figured out how I could have gone through a contract where all of the actors were the writers. You can make a deal through the unions that way. That's what they do with variety acts on television. Rather than paying five individuals to go on and do their act, they pay the L.A. Connection. That's cheaper than paying five individuals. Maybe I could have found a way to cut out the Writers Guild and maybe have done it for the $250K, or tried to. Plus, at the time of the Warner Bros. deal, too, I didn't know if *Mad Movies with the L.A. Connection* was going to get picked up for a second season at that point.

In June, 1986, David Wharton of the *Los Angeles Times* reported, "*Mad Movies with the L.A. Connection* is halfway through its first season. The show is being aired on forty-five independent television stations across the country. It has received favorable reviews in several cities and, in Detroit, garnered surprisingly high ratings for the first several airings. But elsewhere, the ratings have not been as good as the television stations, or the troupe, had hoped. Program directors at six stations from Boston to Seattle said they were not planning on scheduling the show another season.

"Executives at Four Star International said they doubt that they will contract L.A. Connection for another year's worth of series. 'I'm not discounting the concept. I know the humor is terrific,' said Dick

Signarelli (*sic*), Four Star's President of Distribution. But, Signarelli said, *Mad Movies with the L.A. Connection* does not work as well on television as it does live in the theater. 'One-on-one, with the viewer and the television, something is lost.'"[32]

"Stations didn't know what to do with it; it bounced all around the schedule," says Kurt Gardner. "Aside from a small cult of enthusiasts, audiences didn't know what to make of it. It was just a few years too early to catch the cable wave that *Mystery Science Theater 3000* benefited from. Admittedly, the budget was pretty low. Higher production values and more money for promotion certainly could have helped. I also think it was too short; an hour format might have worked better to get the concept across."

Skov adds, "At that time, the executives at Four Star were beginning to disperse and the company was going to be sold. So, they didn't have the same kind of driving force they once had. Dick Cignarelli was our biggest cheerleader and once he decided to leave we knew that we weren't going to get picked back up."

"I think the people at Four Star were hoping that this show plus a few other things they were doing were going to revitalize the company," says Bob Buchholz. "And, a show like that, it's kind of like a *South Park* thing where it takes a little while for it to catch on before you get people following it like a cult thing. It would certainly take a season or two or three to get people talking about it. Plus, in today's age, you put something like that out on the air and you've got people talking about it on social networks. Back then, unless you told your friends, no one knew much about it. It was syndicated so there wasn't a lot of mainstream advertising for it. Also, this was before VCRs so there wasn't much opportunity for people to tape it."

Randy Ridges explains, "My understanding is that the people at Four Star just didn't see the numbers; it was all financial to them. They didn't see the return on the investment that they expected. We thought they could have done a better job in marketing while they claimed that it was a hard show to sell. It's a pretty common story in distribution: the producer has one idea, the distributor has another. There wasn't a lot of support from Four Star and they just didn't renew the contract."

Connie Sue Cook remembers, "When they came in and started measuring the office I thought, *I know we're not getting a new desk*, but no one wanted to say for sure."

1986 also saw the troupe producing a trailer for the Landmark theater chain and making their first of three appearances on *The Midday Show* with Ray Martin in Australia.

A year after *Mad Movies with the L.A. Connection* finished its run, the show found new life when Nickelodeon picked it up for the show for two years of reruns as part of its Nick at Nite line-up. "All of a sudden, it was their most popular show. We were getting more good reviews and more people were starting to talk about it again," says Skov. Most of today's *Mad Movie with the L.A. Connection* fans caught saw the show in its Nick at Nite slot. After the Nick at Nite run, MTV purchased the show for another three year stint from 1989-1991.

In 1988, Kevin Brass of the *Los Angeles Times* reported that "silliness has become a lucrative venture for the comedy group, now known as the unofficial kings of movie dubbing. . . .They recently completed a video for Orion Home Video, *Crocodile Gandhi*, and signed a five-picture deal with Pinnacle pictures to produce movies for theatrical release. The group also has a verbal agreement to do a segment for Eddie Murphy's pilot for NBC."[33]

In truth, the L.A. Connection "wrote a script that involved dubbing and live comedy but it was never bought so the five-picture deal was based on the first one being sold. *Crocodile Gandhi* was a dubbed version of *Hercules Goes to New York* (AKA *Hercules Goes Bananas* Arnold Schwarzenegger's first film). The producers could not continue to pay us and just took our script and tried to do it on their own to no success.

Some of the L.A. Connection could be seen or heard through other outlets in the mid-to-late-1980s. Cast members appeared on *The All Star Comedy Hour.* "We did some spots for *At the Movies* when Rex Reed and Dixie Whatley hosted it. Heck, we even did some industrial films for Northrop, Baxter Pharmaseal, and Southern California Edison," says Skov.

The L.A. Connection was part of the first full season of Fox TV in 1990, with their segment on the ill-fated comedy show *Haywire*, which consisted of two to three-minute clips of several films that had been on *Mad Movies with the L.A. Connection*.

A few of the new jokes for the clips were too racy for even the lenient Fox censors. "I got censored once when I wrote a blow job joke, and it was too far. They said, 'You can't do this.' So, I had to write an alternate joke. I also had to write an alternate joke for Bob Hope [in *My Favorite Brunette*] once because we called a guy a douche bag. Fox didn't like that. *Now* we could have gotten away with it but then it was too much. So, we did an enema joke instead with Bob screwing up the words to "99 Bottles of Beer on the Wall"; 'I'm gonna take those bottles and give you a beer enema.'

In early 1991, Skov signed on to produce the "Deesville" segment of *Into the Night Starring Rick Dees*, which Aleene MacMinn of the *Los Angeles Times* described as a "Mary Hartman-style show-within-a-show segment."[34] The segment had Skov playing a character called "Dead-eye Dick, the Dead Detective," who had a lamp post attached to his back and a bullet hole in his forehead.

"I was kind of like the host of things; no one would see me because I was invisible. One of the things I did was write a bunch of dick jokes. You know, I'd say, 'I'm Dead-Eye Dick the Dead Dick; the dick that's dead; the deadest dick west of the Dakotas; the dead dick.' That would go on and I'd say probably about fifteen dick jokes like that because I knew I'd be censored and the censors would cut half of them out. That left the other half still in. Of course, I ended up playing really stupid. 'What are you talking about?' 'Dick' is another word for detective.' 'I'm just calling myself a dick.' I'd do it with a straight face.

"Playing like you don't know what they are talking about really works sometimes. Just going, 'We're talking about his noodle.' 'Yeah, but isn't the noodle his dick?' 'No, it's his noodle.' 'What is his noodle?' 'I don't know. It just sounds funny, so we're calling it his noodle. You know? Don't touch my noodle!' 'What does that mean?' 'You figure it out. I don't think it should be censored. It's noodle.' And finally they would just leave and we're all laughing because these guys bought this stuff. It really works, and you know what you're doing, but you just don't want to get censored so you figured out ways to do that.

"Sometimes I wrote knowing that the censors may come to my door, and I didn't care because all they'd do is take the jokes out. That's all they could ask you to do. As long as they get to my door before

I record it. I don't want to go back in and change something I've recorded. Back with *Mad Movies with the L.A. Connection*, we would have to turn all the scripts into Four Star before they were recorded. And then one of the guys would come and look at that, and I only remember them coming, I think, once to the office and saying that we went too far on this script. You know what? I can't even remember what script it was.

"Yes, I've had the censors censor me, but probably any writer who ever wrote for television has probably told you the same thing. I mean, unless you're writing for kids, and even then you could probably get censored, but, yeah, I like to push the edge. Sex will relate to everybody, you know, anybody who has ever had it. Put it that way. I mean, little kids aren't going to get it, but let's say we wrote over their heads but you always have to have some of that in there because that drives everything. That drives a lot of movies and television, all that because even in sitcoms there's still sexual tension and energy."

Into the Night (the show's revised name as of July, 1991) didn't last very long. While *Thicke of the Night* ranks as #6 on the Top 10 Late-Night TV Talk Show Bombs list. Dees's show only gets a Dishonorable Mention.[35] Meanwhile, Ken Tucker of *Entertainment Weekly* dismissed the show as "pretty lame."[36]

Blobermouth

Work on *Blobermouth* began in 1989. The project ostensibly capitalized on the release of the 1988 Chuck Russell remake of the 1956 Irvin S. Yeaworth Jr. film. Produced by the Jack H. Harris, who also produced the original film, as well as the bizarre *Beware! The Blob* in 1972, *Blobermouth* pits aspiring stand-up comedian Steve McQueen against the alien blob who has been given a cartoon mouth and an endless stream of Henny Youngman jokes.

"Originally, I reached out to Jack Harris to rent *The Blob*," says Skov. "He'd come to the live shows and I'd interview him at the beginning of the show. *The Blob* was huge for us. It'd sell out all 500 seats. Part of it was because it had a bigger name. Even though it was culty, it wasn't a big cult. It was in color, it had Steve McQueen who wasn't that far-removed from peoples' minds.

The cast recording an episode.

"Harris and I started to get friendlier. We'd go out for lunches. He liked his martinis. I got to be friends with his wife and we did a couple of events with her. Jack and I started talking about making a film project out of it someday. He said that he'd finance the movie but I had to pay for the voiceovers. So, I paid for the talent which I think was about $15,000 for them and the studio time. I gave them either $1,000 or they could get a percentage of the movie. Jack told me that he spent about $125,000. I don't know if it's made any money back but I've never seen any profit. It was worth it, though, and it's another thing where, if people want to find the history of the L.A. Connection, they've got that.

"It was great meeting the producer Jack Harris and his wife," says Steve Pinto. "They were really nice people and easy to work with, she was especially lovely. I wanted to do the best I could for them. Bob Buchholz and Frances Kelly played the leads. I was the Swedish doctor and a few others. The doctor was fun to play. Since this was another cult classic, we wanted to do the best. One of the characters is a fireman in a white turnout coat and white helmet. We made him the Pope. Why? He was dressed in white. The Pope made a cameo appearance."

Skov continues, "When we recorded we had Henny Youngman in the studio. He had to be eighty-something by that time and he kept falling asleep. Every twenty minutes or so we'd wake him up, saying, 'Henny, wake up! The Blob is going to do one of your jokes!' He'd stir and say, 'Oh, that's funny. Okay, I got to go back to sleep.'"

The film's screenplay is credited to Steve Pinto, Kent Skov, Stephen L. Rollman, and Robert Buchholz with direction by Skov. The voices are all the *Mad Movies with the L.A. Connection* regulars with the addition of Frances Kelly as Vaccine (Jane Martin), Steve's love interest.

"Frances Kelly was a member of the L.A. Connection and that's actually her voice in the film. She sounds like a little girl. She got into voice-over work doing kids. The reason she joined is that she used to come to our live movie dubbings because she was friends with our keyboard player, Matt Davis."

Blobermouth sets the action in Mayberry, with our hero, Steve, trying to convince Sheriff Andy and Deputy Barney to stop Blobermouth from taking the stage and ruining Steve's act. Blobermouth upstages Steve at every turn, an easy thing to do as Steve's act seems to consist mostly of him putting his hands in his pockets and recounting the story-so-far in voice-over. There are also a few bizarre musical breaks and a rap theme song that undoubtedly felt dated even in 1990.

Featuring saltier language and far more sexual innuendo, the film comes closer to capturing the L.A. Connection theatrical experience than *Mad Movies with the L.A. Connection.* The Youngman one-liners induce as many groans as they do laughs ("a vasectomy means never having to say you're sorry") with rim shots peppering the film's new soundtrack.

"*The Blob* was one of my favorites," recalls Bob Buchholz, "the live version. *Blobermouth* was good, too, but there was an example of where I think we fine-tuned it too much. We polished it too much and lost some of the spontaneity that we had live."

Blobermouth was one of the 150 finalists (out of 2,000 entrants) for the American Film Institute Los Angeles International Film Festival in 1991. Despite being one of the *Los Angeles Times*'s "recommendations" for the AFI Fest, the reviewer chided it as "less fun than the original,"[37] while the artistic director for the Chicago International Film Festival, Michael Kutza, dismissed the film with, "They just changed the story by putting words in the Blob's mouth, and they're these terrible Henny Youngman jokes."[38]

Some modern reviewers are ambivalent about the film. "The soundtrack, created from scratch by the L.A. Connection, is nothing to shout about—all the dialogue sounds like it was recorded in an echo chamber. And don't even get me started on the hideous music video interludes and mid film recap of the story (I guess the filmmakers were worried we might have forgotten), which may well be the cheesiest things I've ever seen. . . and it doesn't help that the music sucks, too. Is it stupid? Of course. Is it worth seeing? Certainly, but I'd recommend viewing the original version first."[39]

Dennis Delrogh of the *Village View* had a more considered opinion of the film: "Since *The Blob* could practically function as a midnight movie on its own, one at first questions the point of the L.A. Connection's interference. But the resistance factor is soon overcome, first by the gawky physical grace of early Steve McQueen, then by the film's period-piece alertness, with its warped iconic application of the Eisenhower era, and finally by our actual involvement with its makeshift, superimposed plot . . . More than any other actor, Steve McQueen seems to embody the yearnings and frustrations of growing up in the mal-adjusted 1950s. He may be the screen's most boyish pre-Spielberg action hero—and is certainly its most heartbreaking. It's not unusual to observe him in situations in which he appears to be on the verge of tears. *Blobermouth* takes advantage of McQueen's unrest, generating a running gag out of his invariably putting his hands in his pockets. On a bootless quest for identity, McQueen has always suggested extreme disassociation from his environment and is therefore the ideal actor for a film such as this, which is about, as much as anything else, an existential crisis of entrapment in somebody else's show."[40]

After its festival run, *Blobermouth* had a limited theatrical release in 1992. Image Entertainment released the film on DVD in October, 2000.

GET OUT OF YOUR CAGE...GET OUT OF YOUR CAVE...

**Cordially Invites You and a Guest to
LAC's Wild *Improvision* World Premiere of**

1966

All-new plot, all-new live improv dialogue and sound effects, all new fun!
Prizes for best costumes

Friday, June 19, at 8:00 p.m.
or
Friday, June 19, at 10:00 p.m.

at
The Nuart Theatre
11272 Santa Monica Boulevard, West Los Angeles
RSVP Joyce Crawford
(310) 559-1338

An invitation to get your Bat on.

Batman

Capitalizing on the Tim Burton *Batman* films, the L.A. Connection did a series of shows dubbing the 1966 *Batman the Movie* at the Nuart Theatre in west Los Angeles, the Ken Cinema in San Diego, and the L.A. Connection Comedy Theatre in Sherman Oaks in the late summer of 1992.

The film was cut and re-dubbed to have Batman and Robin throwing a party that's crashed by Catwoman, the Joker, the Riddler, and the Penguin. "Even more than the plot, the satirical asides on topics such as Dan Quayle's spelling abilities, backups on the San Diego Freeway and the ineptitude of local cable companies aim to keep the laughs coming."[41]

One of the new voices for the *Batman* show included Jeff Nimoy, who had joined the L.A. Connection after moving out from New York a few months prior. "I was a fan of them from *Thicke of the Night*," Nimoy recalls.

"After a while there were original members of the group but a lot of people had left. I would replace people from the original cast that had left like *Wrestling Women Versus the Aztec Mummy*. However, I was in the original cast for *Batman* and helped originate it. I wrote probably 50 percent or more of that one. I played both Robin and The Penguin. I was doing Burgess Meredith's voice, but doing him like he was in *Rocky*.

"Kent and I wrote that one. He was Batman and I was Robin. We wrote it for ourselves, pretty much; we tailored it to our sense of humor."

At one screening at the L.A. Connection Comedy Theater, director Leslie Martinson and actress Lee Meriwether (Catwoman) made an appearance. Martinson related behind-the-scene stories of the film's production, while Meriwether participated in a "cat's meow" contest with the audience. The troupe injected some much-appreciated ribald humor into the camp classic ("I need to be alone now. I have to go breast-feed my cat," says Catwoman).

"Doing a good job of lip-syncing and creating a believable but nutty story line are the most important facets of dubbing movies,"

Skov says. The stories are mostly scripted beforehand, though some room is left for improvised dialogue, and rehearsed for hours to get the lip-syncing just right. "The whole process takes about thirty or forty hours," Skov calculates. He considers the features successful "if we can make people forget the original movie and get into our plot."[42]

"We did *Batman* at the Nuart Theater, where we did most of them," remembers Nimoy. "And then we decided to put in a screen at the L.A. Connection Theater itself. We started doing a midnight show and we probably did *Batman* for three months straight—maybe longer—every Friday at midnight. The other movies became more like events; you'd do two or three performances of them, one at the Nuart in Santa Monica and then you'd go to San Diego and do one or two nights the next weekend.

"We got to know *Batman* so well that we started improvising more and more during the show. At one point, it really came down to trying to make each other laugh because we had heard it all before. We knew what worked with an audience, so we would do that and for everything else we would just try to bust each other up."

The year also saw the L.A. Connection signing on for a Fox-TV special, *National Lampoon's After School* (not to be confused with the 2003 film *National Lampoon's Barely Legal,* which had the title, *National Lampoon's After School Special,* before release), and doing a weekly radio show, *The L.A. Connection's Interactive Comedy Radio Show*, for KGIL 1260AM. Episodes ran at midnight on Saturdays, where, like the show Terry Thoren listened to in Denver, the L.A. Connection provided an improvised soundtrack for television shows during their time slot. The next year, they had a thirteen-episode run on KIEV 830AM, where Kent Skov re-teamed with his radio friend Norman Davis.

"We would have the radio station take us off delay," says Jeff Nimoy, "and just channel surf. We'd tell people, 'Okay, we're on Channel 11 now, we're on *Star Trek,* and we're going to dub it live.' *Star Trek* was on every Saturday night, and eventually we started looking up to see what episode would be on and we would rent that episode to figure out what time a certain scene we wanted to dub was on. I remember that 'The Doomsday Machine' episode was a good one. I played William Shatner."

Why did Nimoy do Kirk's voice rather than Spock's? "I did a great Kirk, I don't really sound like my cousin, Leonard."

Promotional photos for the A&E Mystery.

Movie Madness Mystery

In August, 1993, *Variety* reported that "Sherman Oaks-based improv troupe L.A. Connection has signed with Arts & Entertainment to produce an hour long special with an option for up to twelve more. The Nov. 18 special, *Movie Madness Mystery with the L.A. Connection,* will feature a dubbed version of 1945 Sherlock Holmes pic, *The Woman in Green.*"[43]

At the time, the L.A. Connection had gotten numerous less-than-stellar reviews. Critics panned their shows as "missing sense of craftsmanship from the actors,"[44] where "the ideas—more often than not—just don't flow."[45]

"Out of all the work that I think we've done so far," Skov says, "I think, the A&E show is the best dubbing show we've ever done. We recorded in front of a live audience, so it's more like how we started. The laughs were real laughter from real people, not a laugh track. There's something about that that, the adrenaline just is so flying high, and it's pure pleasure.

"We did the show twice and tried to bring in a different audience for each one. We had a larger audience for the first show; the theater was packed. The second show was about two-thirds full. Both were very well-received, but the majority of stuff we used was from the first take. The second take was a back-up in case we made any mistakes the first time. We didn't bring anybody back into the studio to fix anything, because overdubbing wouldn't have sound the same. Really, *Movie Madness Mystery with the L.A. Connection* is a pretty close rendition to what it felt like when we did live performances. I think that's why it was so well-received.

"We did some extra things in post, but not much. Maybe I had to slide a voice a little bit. The lip sync was slightly off or I may have had to enhance a few laughs or clapping; minimal stuff. There's so much natural clapping and laughter.

"When we were doing *Mad Movies with the L.A. Connection,* we'd have to sit through the whole cut. Like everything you wanted, you had to watch it be in place, whereas nowadays, you can say, 'Okay, how much of this you want? You want it in here and out here?'

Movie Madness Mystery with the L.A. Connection was the first time we worked nonlinear. The first day the editor did something like that I just stared at him and said, 'What? What? I don't have to watch this whole thing?' And he goes, 'Man, you got to get in the twenty-first century.' It had only been maybe three years since I had been in a studio, and in that time it had all changed so much."

The writers and performers on *Movie Madness Mystery with the L.A. Connection* included the five core writers from *Mad Movies with the L.A. Connection,* along with Julienne Dallara and Jeff Nimoy. "It was a pretty good collaboration," says Nimoy. "Everybody added quite a bit but I'd say that Bob [Buchholz], Kent, myself, and Connie probably wrote the bulk of it. Steve Pinto was having an off show. Usually he's great but, writing-wise, he couldn't get it together for that show.

"I don't know who picked *The Woman in Green* but it was probably Kent. I actually came up with the premise for that one, the storyline of Smoke Stoppers and trying to get people to stop smoking. Then we went from there.

"Bob played Sherlock Holmes, and I played Watson," says Nimoy. "Bob just had that perfect leading man voice. He was just great at that stuff. For the A&E cast, Kent took the *Mad Movies with the L.A. Connection* cast and added me, probably because of our work on *Batman* together. And, he also threw in his wife, mostly for politics."

"Julienne Dallara was my wife at the time," recounts Skov. "I met her in 1991. I had gotten invited to an actor's showcase; I was working for Rick Dees at ABC at the time. I used to get a lot of invitations because people thought I was some kind of big-time producer but I was just doing a segment on Rick Dees. I got invited to meet this other girl and she was kind of homely, not my type, but I remember seeing Julienne and thinking she was very sexy. She played a nerd in half of the showcase and a real sex pot in the other half. I went to their party afterwards and she memorized my phone number at ABC and called me the next day. We started dating and I got engaged to her maybe five or six months later."

Skov was both director and head writer for the show. "I was kind of like a bull, you know. I rehearsed these guys, overly rehearsed them so they could do this thing backward and forward, and, when it came to game day, we were always good. And we had to be because when we first started doing it, it was kind of like just a fun thing, but then the demand of our audiences expected a higher quality. And also we had buyers, so every time we'd do a show, at least locally, there was somebody out there that would actually want to buy our stuff or offer us a job, or give us stuff. I think it culminated with that one show. We wanted to make it our masterpiece.

"At that point, we had been doing it for eleven years. Eleven years of hard work with this same cast of people. We'd been in the trenches a long time together, we knew how each other wrote, and it was just a real pleasure to do that show because I think that was the last hurrah for the *Mad Movies with the L.A. Connection* cast, and obviously we went out with a very bright light. It was fantastic."

"They called it a 'back end pilot,'" says Nimoy. "They say it's a special because if the ratings do well and they like it, they'll order more and turn it into a series."

Skov adds, "A&E weren't sure, at the time, which direction they wanted to go. They were doing *An Evening at the Improv* and more stand-up comedy. Second City was the first hour of the two-hour block we were in. A&E promoted the hell out of Second City because they had the name recognition and we kind of rode on their fan base along with whatever people came to watch us. A&E decided to go in an entirely different direction. Now it's *Duck Dynasty* land."

Fittingly, *Movie Madness Mystery with the L.A. Connection* earned A&E a CableAce Award nomination for Best Comedy Special in 1994.

"I think A&E had already passed on it before it was nominated," says Nimoy. "The CableAce thing was all me. I was pissed off that they passed on what I thought was a great show so I said, 'Let's show them and let's nominate ourselves for a CableAce Award.' I did all the legwork; I made copies of it, I found out where to get the application and filled that out, and lo and behold, we got a nomination. They only gave us two tickets to the CableAce Awards show and, even though I got us the nomination, Kent went with his wife and I got shut out of the show. But, that's okay. We lost. I would have been pissed if we'd won and I wasn't there. I think we lost to *Mr. Bean*."

"Around 1994 or 1995, most of the main guys began to get work and move on," says Skov. "They'd been with me for thirteen to

COSTUME DESIGN

Thierry Bosquet
"Capriccio"
BRAVO Cable Network

Deborah Everton
"Heart of Darkness"
Turner Network Television

Judy Pepperdine
"Miss Marple: The Mirror Cracked from Side to Side"
Arts & Entertainment Network

Richard LaMotte
"The Broken Chain"
Turner Network Television

Joan Wadge
"The House of Eliott"
Arts & Entertainment Network

COMEDY SPECIAL

"A Year's Worth with Will Durst"
Arts & Entertainment Network
Tim Braine, Executive Producer
Michael Katz, Executive Producer
Rick Siegel, Executive Producer
Steve Natt, Supervising Producer
Phil Gurin, Producer
Leslyle Gustat, Producer
Joe Michaels, Producer
Rich Procter, Producer
Nancy Swaim, Producer

"Jocks"
Comedy Central
Tim Braine, Executive Producer
Kevin Meagher, Executive Producer
Ted Schachter, Executive Producer
David Steinberg, Executive Producer
Steve Natt, Producer

"Merry Christmas, Mr. Bean"
Home Box Office
Tiger Aspect Productions
Peter Bennett-Jones, Executive Producer
Sue Vertue, Producer
John Birkin, Director
Rowan Atkinson, Writer
Richard Curtis, Writer
Robin Driscoll, Writer

"Movie Madness Mystery with the L.A. Connection"
Arts & Entertainment Network
L.A. Connection
Kent Skov, Executive Producer

STAND-UP COMEDY SPECIAL

"HBO Comedy Half-Hour: Chris Rock"
Home Box Office
Production Partners, Inc.
Chris Rock, Executive Producer/Performer
Tom Bull, Producer
Sandy Chanley, Producer
Keith Truesdell, Director

"HBO Comedy Half-Hour: D.L. Hughley"
Home Box Office
Production Partners, Inc.
D.L. Hughley, Performer
Sandy Chanley, Executive Producer
Tom Bull, Producer
Keith Truesdell, Director

"HBO Comedy Half-Hour: Eddie Griffin"
Home Box Office
Production Partners, Inc.
Eddie Griffin, Performer
Sandy Chanley, Executive Producer
Tom Bull, Producer
Keith Truesdell, Director

"HBO Comedy Half-Hour: Margaret Cho"
Home Box Office
Production Partners, Inc.
Margaret Cho, Performer
Sandy Chanley, Executive Producer
Tom Bull, Producer
Keith Truesdell, Director

"HBO Comedy Half-Hour: Suzanne Westenhoefer
Home Box Office
Moffitt-Lee Productions
Suzanne Westenhoefer, Performer
John Moffitt, Executive Producer/Director
Pat Tourk Lee, Executive Producer
Juliet Blake, Producer
Trevor Hopkins, Producer
Nancy Kurshner, Line Producer

PERFORMANCE IN A COMEDY SPECIAL

Rowan Atkinson
"Merry Christmas, Mr. Bean"
Home Box Office

Torian Hughes
"Montreal International Comedy Festival '94"
Showtime

Dennis Miller
"The State of the Union: Undressed"
Comedy Central

Tracey Ullman
"Tracey Ullman: Takes on New York"
Home Box Office

Nominees for the CableAce Awards.

fifteen years. It was sad to see them go but it was good to see that they were successful. Steve Pinto stayed with me. Otherwise, it took a while to build back up – a good ten years before I started having really good performers I could use in that same capacity again.

"Julienne and I were married for about eight years, but it's kind of a sad story. She got mellitus in 1996, which paralyzed her from the waist down. We had two kids and the second kid was six months old when that happened. It was really kind of devastating; it was a tough time for all of us.

"The dubbing really slowed down. You've got to have the team that you can do the voice-over work with, and help you do the writing. I tend to write much better if I have a partner because I bounce stuff off the other person; that kind of brings out the improvisational element that I have. I mean, I write stuff by myself, and I've done writing, but it helps me if I have something to work from. That's why I think the dubbing helps a little bit, because if I see a clip, that gets me halfway into the brains of what I am going to write versus not having anything, writing from scratch."

In 1995, the L.A. Connection signed a deal with Universal Theme Parks. People waiting in line at Sea World could pass the time watching *Mad Movies with the L.A. Connection.* The troupe was also featured as part of the Incredibly Strange Film Festival in Atlanta, Georgia. They had three shows on May 6, performing with *Plan 9 from Outer Space* and *Attack of the 50-foot Woman* at the Variety Playhouse.

The following year, they signed with the USA Network's Sci-Fi channel to develop *Crash Buster*. "We were going to dub episodes of *Flash Gordon.* The thing with Julienne made it hard on me; she worked on *Crash Buster* with me, Jeff Nimoy, and a couple other people. It was a pretty funny presentation we had for them but then they got *Mystery Science Theater 3000* from Comedy Central. Since they already had a following, Sci-Fi didn't want to have both of us." *Mystery Science Theater 3000* ran for two years on Sci-Fi from 1997 to 1999. "I think that was one of their last attempts at trying to do any comedy on that channel," muses Skov.

"Julienne could still do some voice-over work with me, but I couldn't work as much. I had to stop doing stuff for about four years; just trying to take care of my two kids and my family. Eventually we kind of grew apart and got divorced."

"Julienne got remarried and I got remarried. We have a decent relationship with each other still. Of course, we both still take care of both the kids together. That was probably our best production; producing those two kids."

The late 1990s also brought appearances on the *Home and Family Show* on the Family Channel, shows for Xerox, Chrysler, the Southern California Cable Association, and a commercial for California prunes.

Many of the *Mad Movies with the L.A. Connection* cast continued to work in dubbing. Bob Buchholz works with South American and Korean movies, dubbing them into English. "He uses the lip synching and phonetics to take movies and rewrite them a bit so you don't change the story too much but match the lips better," says Skov.

"One of the other guys, Jeff Nimoy, went on to do *Digimon* and do the same thing, taking Japanese words and translating them into English while matching the lip synch."

Mad Movies in the 21st Century

By the year 2000, VHS was on the decline and would be usurped by DVD a few years hence. The window for physical media was closing with YouTube a scant five years from creation. The year also brought the *Maddest Movies 2000 & Beyond Direct Video Club*.

The press release describes it as an "exclusive offer is available for 130 half-hour Episode Collectors Editions." The first 2,000 people to sign up were to receive an introductory price of $390 (plus tax, of course) for a full year of twenty-six half-hour episodes. With anyone after those initial 2,000 having to shell out $495. Episodes would come with outtakes, original footage, and "souvenir treats." People could sign up to purchase episodes anywhere from one to five years.

The subscription service would have included 130 new episodes. "Among the titles Skov has lined up for the new series: *High School Caesar, Summer City* with Mel Gibson, *The People* with William Shatner, *Murder in Music City* with Sonny Bono, and episodes of *Dragnet* and *Ozzie and Harriet*. No longer protected by copyright, they're fair game."[46]

"Since it costs approximately $30,000 per episode to produce, and Skov and his group are producing the first tape [in September, 2000], they need a solid subscription base to bankroll their ambitious efforts."[47]

Unfortunately, Skov was unable to get enough people interested. "It was too expensive, really. I spent $5,000 on a PR company for a campaign to try and get it going. I got some radio and newspaper coverage. CNN did a story on it. But I just couldn't get enough. I retained all of the e-mails of the people who signed up or were interested. Of course, as time went on, those e-mails aren't any good anymore because people changed their addresses.

"Of all the e-mail addresses we've collected," Skov continues, "maybe we have 150 that still work. That's a start. But what I'd like to do is accumulate about 10,000 solid names of people who'd like to buy our stuff. These days we might be able to create episodes for $25,000 apiece. Back in 1985, it cost us $35,000 to do them because of the studios, the guild costs, and all these expenses.

"We started coming back and doing live dubbing again around 2004 at Cineplex, a local dinner and a movie kind of place. We did that for maybe a year or two before we realized it was too pricey for our clientele. We went to the Cinespace and lowered our prices. Now, we had a huge draw because we don't price people out of the ballpark. We keep everything at good pricing so that people want to see what we do.

"That's when the second wave of the *Mad Movies with the L.A. Connection* began to take hold. We began to get a new following. With the advent of YouTube, people started posting it on there and they were getting thousands of hits. When they caught a guy selling 840,000 bootleg copies, I went, 'Geez, okay. They're out there still.' I was getting e-mails on a regular basis from people wanting to buy it from me, and I couldn't sell it to them. I didn't have the rights.

"I went down to Fox to try and secure them. I had one guy who was a real champion of it. He was really excited about re-releasing them, putting out a box set of them, even making new ones. Then he found that 20th Century Fox owned *Mad Movies with the L.A. Connection*, not Fox Television. He couldn't do a thing except send me over to another department, where I couldn't get anyone to tell me the time of day.

"20th Century was all these film guys, not TV guys. TV was the low end of what they do. They don't give a crap about old shows, especially since they never owned it, they didn't make it, and they weren't invested in it in like Four Star was. They only acquired it when they bought the Four Star library. We were just thrown in with everything else.

"Finally, they sent me to the marketing guy. He just sat there, looking at me, and said, 'I don't know why they sent you here.' He says, 'Quite frankly, between you and me, they don't sell any of their stuff. They're in the business of acquiring products. They don't want to sell their product. They may license it, so you can go make something, but they would retain the rights to the original. It won't happen.' I kind of gave it up; just kind of forgot about it for a while.

"They're not going to give me the rights. Period. I had people that really seriously wanted to buy it and I could have packaged it and sold it. This was still when physical media was viable. You could sell a lot more then than you could do today.

"I still keep getting e-mails, and people going, 'No one is going to know if you send me copy. Come on. File sharing, you know.' I'm not about to go to jail because I'm sending people a *Mad Movies with the L.A. Connection*. It's just not worth it for me. I have contracts and I honor my contracts."

The L.A. Connection introduced a new film into their live repertoire in 2005 with *Hercules Goes to New York*. Says Skov, "Then we made a new version of *Night of the Living Dead* in 2006. We were starting to make a few new things and, at the same time, I was cementing my relationship with my new writing partner. We work well together, writing fast and funny. He's probably as good of a writing partner as I've had.

"Doing these new movies also secured all the voices. So, if I get another show, I'm surrounded by some really good voices and talent now that I feel like I can rival a *Mad Movie with the L.A. Connection* type show again, because I've got the talent around me. And you just have to wait for your time. It's unfortunate it took me almost thirty years. In that time I've learned that you just have to keep going at it and trying."

End Notes

1 "Oddballs in the Tubes' Bullpen" by Robert Hilburn, *Los Angeles Times*, 1977.

2 "Group Improvises New Comedy Style" by Greg Braxton, *Los Angeles Times*.

3 Ibid.

4 "Getting New Laughs Out of Old Movies" by Jon Matsumoto, Los Angeles Times, July 20, 1994.

5 "Comedy Group Attacks Big Film Project" by Diana L. Chapman, *Los Angeles Times*, November 19, 1982.

6 "For Late-Night and Thicke, Things Are Wearing Thin" by Lawrence Christon.

7 "Movie Rip-Offs: A User's Guide – Détournement and Dub Parodies" by Sean Welsh, *The Physical Impossibility of Rad in the Mind of Someone Bogus* blog, May 21, 2011 http://physicalim-possibility.wordpress.com/2011/05/22/movie-rip-offs-a-users-guide-detournement-and-dub-parodies

8 The SCTV Guide http://www.sctvguide.ca/episodes/sctv_s3.htm#Show_25

9 All evidence seems to point to *What's Up Hideous Sun Demon* having a 1983 release date, not 1989 as reported by Michael R. Pitts in *Horror Film Stars* (McFarland & Company, 2002). However, other signs point to a later date such as the report in the November 22, 1990 edition of *The Deseret News* that "Jay Leno will provide the voice of the title character in the redubbed, camped-up version of the '50s B-film" ("Outtakes – Old Creatures, New Features).

10 *The Encyclopedia of Martial Arts Movies* by Bill Palmer, Scarecrow Press, 1995.

11 All quotes from Lloyd Kaufman from the Troma VHS release of *Ferocious Female Freedom Fighters*.

12 Sources put the release date for *Membakar Matahari* anywhere from 1981 to 1984.

13 And, perhaps, Kent Skov's multiple appearances on the popular "The Midday Show" in Australia.

14 "Herco the Magnificent" appeared on Season 1 episode 6. "Gidget Goes Tasmanian" on Season 2 episode 4.

15 "Double Take turns corn into laughs" Author Unknown, *The Age*, February 3, 1989.

16 "Killer Bee Movie" by Dominic Cavendish, *The Independent*, December 8, 1993.

17 "Making of: Hercules Returns" by Andrew L. Urban, *Urban Cinefile*, http://www.urbancinefile.com.au

18 "David Parker" by Peter Malone, *Peter Malone's website*, September 10, 1998, http://petermalone.misacor.org.au

19 Hercules Returns program notes, http://history.sundance.org/films/1490/hercules_returns

20 "Twisted Flicks on the Seattle Channel" YouTube Video https://www.youtube.com/watch?v=Ael8lq2Y9E0

21 "Chop Phooey! No Art in Painful, Brainless Martial Arts Spoof" by Jonathan Foreman, *New York Post*, January 26, 2002.

22 "Review: 'Kung Pow Enter the Fist'" by Eddie Cockrell, *Variety*, January 26, 2002.

23 "Bad Lip Reading: behind the viral videos everyone's talking about" by Melissa Bell, *The Washington Post*, October 18, 2011.

24 "NBC To Broadcast 'Tonight,' 'Late Night' in Stereo" by Stephen Advokat, Knight-Ridder Newspapers, June 28, 1985.

25 "Adventures in Television Syndication" by Kurt Gardner, *Weird Movie Village* blog, June 7, 2009.

26 "Writers Guild Has 127G Beef with Four-Star" by Staff Writer, *Variety Daily*, April 24, 1986.

27 "The L.A. Connection" by Theda K. Reichman, *The Valley Entertainer*, November 1985.

28 "Records show man confessed to killing" Associated Press, *The Prescott Courier*, April 18, 1993.

29 "Nightmare on Elm Drive" by Dominic Dunne, *Vanity Fair*, October 1990.

30 Howard Rosenberg, "'Twas a Season for Scandals-- and Even Secrets", *Los Angeles Times*, January 01, 1988.

31 "Cable Casting" *Broadcasting*, Vol. 108 No 3, January 21, 1985.

32 "Comic Troupe Still Trying to Make the Connection" by David Wharton, *Los Angeles Times*, June 26, 1986.

33 "L.A. Comedy Group Makes Film Dubbing an Art Form" by Kevin Brass, *Los Angeles Times*, July 22, 1988.

34 "Television" by Aleen MacMinn, *Los Angeles Times*, April 19, 1991.

35 "Top 10 Late-Night TV Talk Show Bombs" by Chris Holmes, Pop Dose, popdose.com/top-10-late-night-tv-talk-show-bombs, September 4, 2013

36 "Into the Night Starring Rick Dees" by Ken Tucker, Entertainment Weekly, August 3, 1990.

37 "Today At AFI Festival" Compiled by Michael Wilmington, *Los Angeles Times*, April 19, 1991.

38 "A World of Film Comes To Chicago" by Mark Caro, *The Chicago Tribune*, October 11, 1991.

39 "Blobermouth" by Adam Groves http://www.fright.com/edge/blobermouth.htm

40 "Blobering at the Mouth" by Dennis Delrogh, *Village View*, April 24-30, 1992.

41 "Dubbing the Dynamic Duo" by Ruth Stroud, *Los Angeles Times*, August 07, 1992.

42 Ibid.

43 "Short Takes" by Variety Staff, *Variety*, August 11, 1993.

44 "Comedy That Doesn't Quite Cut It" by Ray Loynd, *Los Angeles Times*, December 24, 1993.

45 "Sketchy Night of Comedy" by Robert Koehler, *Los Angeles Times*, January 8, 1993.

46 "Comic Plans Revival on Tape" by John Hartl, *Seattle Times*, August, 11, 2000.

47 "Series Goofs on Classic Films" by Michael Blowen, *Boston Globe*, August 27, 2000.

Kent Skov

www.ingramcontent.com/pod-product-compliance
Lightning Source LLC
Chambersburg PA
CBHW060541100426

42742CB00013B/2410